Ensl

BS 3/21

KT-559-643

EMILY VAUGHN
MY TRUE STORY OF SURVIVAL

WITH VERONICA CLARK

Enslaved

HARPER
element

Certain details in this story, including names, places and dates,
have been changed to protect privacy.

HarperElement
An imprint of HarperCollins*Publishers*
1 London Bridge Street
London SE1 9GF

www.harpercollins.co.uk

HarperCollins*Publishers*
1st Floor, Watermarque Building, Ringsend Road
Dublin 4, Ireland

First published by HarperElement 2021

1 3 5 7 9 10 8 6 4 2

A catalogue record of this book is
available from the British Library

ISBN 978-0-00-841594-5

Printed and bound in Great Britain by
CPI Group (UK) Ltd, Croydon

MIX
Paper from
responsible sources
FSC™ C007454

For 'Lily'

I would like to dedicate this book to my daughter
'Lily', who gave me a reason to carry on even
when times were tough.

CHAPTER ONE

DRUG RUNNER

The white van was cramped and uncomfortable. The thick air was stale inside and it stank of long-smoked cigarettes, which carpeted the floor – a pattern of twisted peach-coloured fag butts and dustings of grey ash. Barry cursed as a car pulled sharply to a halt in front, the traffic lights flashing from amber to red.

'Fuck's sake!' he swore. Twisting sideways in his seat, he turned to look at me. ''Ere, pass us a fag will you, Em?'

I grabbed the metallic Lambert & Butler cigarette packet. The small, silver box caught against the light as I wrapped my fingers around its corners. The silky outer wrapper slipped against my palm as I stretched out my fingers and flipped open the top of it.

'Come on, hurry up, I'm gagging here!' Barry complained as my fingers fumbled across the two neatly lined-up rows; each cigarette waiting to be chosen.

His eyes flitted between me and the lights; the van jolted forwards and we began to move again as they changed.

'Here,' he said, throwing me a disposable purple plastic lighter. 'Light one up, will yer?'

I opened my mouth, put the cig between my lips, and clicked the lighter; a golden and blue flame danced in front of my eyes. I nudged the cigarette tip against it, sucking at the end to force it to catch and light. Then I snuffed out the flame and handed both to Barry. As his hand reached out I noticed how filthy his nails were – a ground-in black lined the inside. It looked as though he'd not washed his hands in weeks, which he probably hadn't. I didn't want him to catch me staring so I quickly looked away.

'Good girl,' he said, grinning at me. 'Take one yourself.'

I smiled and repeated the process, lighting the fag and smoking along with Barry until the van had filled with a thick, grey fog that seemed to hang above our heads. I turned and glanced behind me; the back of the van floor was littered with crap – spanners and wrenches, scrunched-up newspapers, copper pipes, discarded cups and food wrappers. In many ways I was glad of the smoke – at least it masked the smell of mouldy, half-eaten burgers. Every time we turned a sharp right the rubbish would slide so that it stacked up against the side of the van. It would settle until we took a sharp left and then it would slam against the opposite side – a continual rattle and smash of junk. The smell of diesel drifted up inside the van, catching against the back of my throat, making me cough.

'You wanna cut down on those,' Barry teased, leaning across to elbow me sharply, waiting for me to get the joke. He bent forward and stabbed a filthy finger against the radio. The van filled with music; it blared out as he tapped his fingers against the steering wheel in time with the song.

I opened up the window to try and breathe in some fresh air; the diesel and smoke had left me feeling sick. Welsh countryside whizzed by outside but I didn't have a clue where we were going. I just hoped and prayed we'd arrive soon so I could get away from the sliding rubbish and rotten stench. Eventually, Barry indicated right and we pulled up in a street full of terraced houses. One of them had a wooden fence painted yellow. It seemed to stand out like a sore thumb against the plainer brown and white ones. The van slowed and creaked as Barry ratcheted on the handbrake.

'Right,' he said, throwing his cigarette to the floor, adding to the cig butt carpet. 'That's it; we're here. Time to get out.'

I felt relieved.

'Where are we?' I asked, immediately regretting it as soon as the words had left my mouth.

He lifted a finger and tapped the side of his nose.

'A man; we're here to see a man. That's all you need to know.'

I followed Barry as he walked up a short flagstone path; his rake-thin legs were buried beneath filthy jeans that hung loosely from his slender frame. He put out an arm and pushed open the front door without knocking. Whoever lived here must have been expecting him, I thought as I followed him inside. The house was small as though all the rooms had been shrunken. There was a set of stairs on the left and a kitchen directly on my right. The main living room was directly in front of us. Inside were chairs, a sofa and, sitting on top, the fattest man I'd ever seen. He was so obese that I couldn't help but stare. I wondered how the small brown sofa managed to hold him up.

'Hi, Baz,' the fat man said in a matter-of-fact voice. He looked to Barry's left and spotted me, lurking in the shadow of the doorway. 'Who's this?'

'Em, it's Emily, but, don't worry, she's a good girl. She won't say nothing, will you, Em?'

Both men looked over as though waiting for an answer, so I shook my head.

'Great!' the overweight man grinned. 'Right, let's get down to business!'

Barry walked over to a coffee table in the middle of the room and stacked up some brown bricks.

'There's nine bars there, Bryn, so let me know how much you want, and I'll cut it and weigh it for you.'

I watched Bryn's fleshy wrist wobble like jelly as he stretched out his hand, picked up one of the solid bricks and gave it a cursory sniff. He inhaled deeply before nodding in agreement. I felt my stomach turn just watching him – he was repulsive. Barry settled down on the sofa next to him.

'Hang on; I've got something else for you, too. They're here somewhere,' he said, checking all around, tapping his jean pockets. He wedged a hand on the sofa and slid it underneath Bryn's arse. Then he burst out laughing. 'That's where they were. You was only sitting on the bastard things!'

Barry continued to laugh and held up two clear plastic bags full of white powder. My eyes darted between the two men. I felt awkward and out of my depth, standing there in the middle of the fat stranger's front room. I took an anxious step backwards to try and fade into the shadows.

'Don't just stand there. Come and sit down,' the man insisted, brushing his fingers against a few strands of hair that looked as though they'd been glued to his bald head. It was obvious he'd combed it that way to conceal his baldness but he was fooling no one. He gestured towards the seat next to him, but that seemed too close and intimate. I crossed the room and plonked myself down in a chair opposite both men. I tried not to gag because, now I was on their level, I could smell the fat one from where I was sitting – a mixture of stale body odour, cigarettes and yeast. I wondered if he had some old food hidden in the mounds of flesh that hung down from his belly. I decided not to breathe in too deeply.

'I'm Bryn, by the way. You wanna fag?' he asked.

I looked over towards Barry; he nodded in confirmation.

'Yeah.'

I decided that I needed a smoke to try and take away the stench.

'Here,' Bryn said, pushing a tin of roll-ups across the table towards me. I lifted the lid and lit one. Then I took a deep drag and watched as the bluish grey smoke rose and curled up into the air like a circling finger.

The room was dark and, even though it was daytime outside, the curtains had been pulled tightly shut. There was a shaft of light peeking in around the edges, but the room was dim with only a side-light switched on. I looked on as Barry began to expertly cut and weigh out the drugs, using a small set of weights and scales.

'What's this heroin like, Barry?' Bryn asked.

'Its good shit, that. Trust me. Your customers are going to love it. I can't get enough.'

Bryn nodded, dabbed his fingers in some of the powder and rubbed them together. The silken dust coated his fat fingers in a talcum powder as he opened up his mouth and rubbed them against his gums. Then he inhaled and breathed out slowly through his nostrils. There was a deep whistling noise as the air struggled to leave his body.

'Not bad, not bad,' he agreed. 'I'll have some of that, too.'

'The usual?' Barry said, raising an eyebrow as though Bryn was sitting inside a restaurant.

'Yep.'

Once the weed, heroin and coke had been divided and bagged up in strips of black plastic, Bryn settled his debt as Barry wrapped the remaining drugs back up. I wasn't sure how much he paid in total but I overheard Barry mutter something about £80 per gram of coke. Bryn pulled out a wad of banknotes and laid them on the table for Barry to count. Once he had he pushed them deep inside his jeans pocket and clambered to his feet. My eyes were still on stalks because I'd never seen so much money in my life.

'Come on, Em, time for us to leave.'

'Bye,' fat Bryn said, giving me a jokey wave as I got up from the chair. I wasn't sure what I should do so I turned away and followed Barry towards the front door but, before he'd opened it Barry turned towards me.

'Put this up your top for me, will you?' he asked, handing me the large packet of drugs.

I did as I was told and pushed the polythene packet up inside my thin jumper to hide it. I realised that's why I was there – to hide drugs in case he got stopped by the police. I'd expected him to give me more instructions but he didn't; instead, with the radio blaring and the rubbish sliding around in the back of the van, we made our way home along the winding country roads towards the Welsh coastline. Eventually we parked up outside his house and I followed Barry inside. We walked into a washroom at the back of the house. I stood and waited as he pulled out a huge, blue metal toolbox from the back of a cupboard.

'Here, put it in here,' he instructed.

Barry pulled the top two handles apart which forced the toolbox to open like a metal mouth. I placed the square packet inside and Barry laid some tools on top before closing it and pushing it back inside the cupboard. I left Barry's and crossed the road to my house as though nothing had happened. I didn't say a word to Mum, who presumed I'd been out on the estate, playing with the other kids. Only I knew the truth.

Barry's step-daughter, Ashley, and I were friends. We lived opposite each other on the estate, which was situated on the outskirts of a nondescript Welsh seaside town. Mine and Ashley's parents – her mum Angela and dad Mike – had been really good friends. They would all go drinking together in the local pub. But then Angela and Mike split, and then her mum met and started going out with Barry. Before long, Barry had all sorts of lengths of copper piping and old radiators that had been propped up in the drive-way. The boilers and radiators were old, rusty and leaking, with missing valves – it looked like the local tip. It annoyed some of the other neighbours, but no one dared say a word because Barry wasn't someone you could complain to or about. Everyone who lived on the estate thought Barry was a plumber; only I knew otherwise. Barry knew lots about fixing boilers, but he made the bulk of his money through dealing drugs. He worked as a plumber alongside another man, called Stan, who lived a few streets away. Plumber or not, people didn't seem to trust Stan with their boilers as much as they trusted Barry.

A few weeks following our trip to fat Bryn's house, Barry was outside, stripping parts from an old boiler he'd propped up against his van on the driveway. It was autumn, but the sun was out and it still felt warm. Ashley and I were busy playing out in the garden, when Mum nipped out for something.

'Lisa!' Barry shouted over, giving her a wave.

'Oh, hi,' she replied, smiling and waving back at him.

'Listen, is it okay if I take your Emily out with our Ashley?'

Although she didn't know Barry as well as she'd known Mick, Mum trusted Angela. Barry was Angela's boyfriend, which meant she trusted him in turn.

'Yeah, okay then. Where are you off to?' she asked, almost as an afterthought.

'Just thought I'd take them for a drive, you know, get them out for a while in the van … what with the weather being so nice,' he said, gesturing up at the sun in the sky.

Mum smiled; if she had any doubts then she didn't voice them. After all, Barry was our neighbour.

'I'll have her tea ready in a few hours.'

'No problem,' Barry said, grinning. 'We'll be back way before then.'

Before she could change her mind, Barry had Ashley and me sitting inside his van. I was in the front and Ashley was crouched down in the back, hanging on to the back of my headrest.

'Everybody ready? Right, let's go!' Barry said as though we were on an adventure. He turned the key in the ignition and the van spluttered and then fired into life.

Our journey went quickly and, before I knew it, we'd pulled up outside a house in the middle of a housing estate miles away from our own. I didn't feel as unsure or nervous as I had last time because this time Ashley was with me. I knew what to expect, or so I thought.

'Listen, girls,' Barry said, pulling four small squares out of a zipped-up bag between us. Each square had been wrapped in black polythene – similar to a bin bag – and sealed with tape. 'I need you to hide these under your tops and take them into that house over there,' he said pointing towards a property with a blue door.

Ashley and I twisted our necks to look through the windscreen.

'See it?'

We both stared through the glass and nodded.

'Great! Now, push these packets underneath your T-shirts. But, whatever you do, don't drop them. It's really important!'

Ashley looked over at her step-father.

'Do we have to knock, you know, on the door?'

'No. Just go in. The man is expecting you.'

I watched Ashley as she lifted up her sweatshirt; she pushed the bags underneath and tucked the bottom of it into the waistband of her jeans. I glanced down at my Miffy T-shirt and did the same. I knew it was drugs because I'd hidden the same only a few weeks earlier at Bryn's house. However, at least that time he'd given me the drugs as we'd left the house, not before we'd gone in. My legs were shaking; I wondered if we were being watched as we climbed down from the van and walked towards the stranger's door.

My heart was thumping with both fear and excitement, as though we were part of a strange game we were acting out. I felt as though I was in a movie. As we approached the blue door, I wondered what we should do if no one answered. Should we knock and wait or turn and climb back into Barry's van? I turned to check he was still there, parked on the opposite side of the road. He was. I faced back towards the door and swallowed my fear. Ashley and I stepped closer. Without warning the door swung open to reveal a thin-looking man with hollowed out cheeks and fine hair. I'd never met him before but he invited us inside. I followed Ashley because she seemed to know what she was doing.

'On the table,' the man ordered in a voice that was neither friendly nor welcoming.

I put my hand up my shirt but held the hem of it down in my other hand because I didn't want him to see my bare chest. With the bags on the table we turned towards the door.

'Hang on,' he called, stopping us both dead in our tracks. 'I need to check it first.'

We watched as he grabbed one of the packets and ripped off the black polythene. There was another one inside but it was clear and full of white powder. He opened the packet, wet a finger in his mouth, and dipped it inside the powder as though it was sherbet. Then he rubbed the finger inside his mouth, just as Bryn had done. I looked over at Ashley, unsure what we were supposed to do. As I did, the man threw back his head and his eyes rolled backwards. After a moment, he composed himself and glanced down at us.

'Okay, you can leave.'

Barry was sitting behind the wheel, waiting for us as we clambered back inside the van. The engine was running and the van shuddered as thick diesel smoke poured out the back of the exhaust pipe.

'All good?' he asked as Ashley climbed over the passenger seat into the back.

'All good,' she responded, nodding.

Barry smiled to himself. Turning the key, he cut off the engine and climbed out of the van.

'Where's he going?' I asked.

'To collect his money.'

We waited for a few minutes. Barry reappeared, blinking against the sunlight as he pushed something inside his jacket pocket. He held a hand against his eyes to try and shield them. Then he checked the coast was clear before walking over to us and the van. He lifted himself back into the driver's seat and, without saying a word, started up the engine and lifted off the handbrake. Then we pulled away, leaving the house with the strange man far behind.

'Well done, girls,' he said a few moments later as we sped along the surrounding country roads. The green fields and hills blurred through the window as we made our way back home. ''Ere, help yourself to fags.'

Ashley grabbed the packet and handed me one before pulling another one out for herself.

'Lighter,' Barry said, throwing it into my lap. I lit mine and then Ashley's cigarettes. We puffed away as he concentrated on the road ahead. The radio was blaring 'Genie in a Bottle' by Christina Aguilera. Barry tapped his fingers as Ashley and I sang along happily at the tops of our voices.

I had just done my first drug run across county lines; I was eleven years old.

CHAPTER TWO

'RINSING' COCAINE

I'd always hated school, and now that Barry had opened my eyes to a whole new and exciting world I hated it with a vengeance.

I had very long brown hair so I stood out, even though I didn't want or mean to. Some of the other kids teased me and called me names so I'd always felt like an outsider – but not any more. Suddenly, my confidence had grown and that was all thanks to one man – Barry. Soon, Ashley and I were out with him in his van all the time. Ashley was only ten – a year younger than me – but Barry would supply us both with fags, sweets or a couple of quid to spend down the shop. The money and my new 'job' made me feel important, as though I'd grown up overnight.

Both inside and outside school I'd become a bit of a handful. My sister Lucy and I had gone through so many babysitters that I'd lost count. In many ways, things had already begun to turn a little strange before that first day Barry had taken me out in his van. Mum and Dad weren't big drinkers but, like most parents, they enjoyed letting their hair down at the weekends. The only problem was

Lucy and I would play up for whichever babysitter they'd brought in for the night. My parents had always enjoyed having drinks with Angela and her ex Mick, and they wanted to continue it with Angela and Barry. Between them, they came up with a plan – they'd hire a babysitter to look after all the kids together. Most teenagers wouldn't come near us because we were known for being a total nightmare; only one was brave enough to step up and take on the challenge and his name was Jonathan. Jon was twenty years old and a bit of a geek. My parents had known him for years because he'd grown up on our estate, so they trusted him. Jon would come over to our house to look after me, Lucy, Ashley and her older sister Beca, who – at thirteen – was a bit older than me. But we were real little sods. One night we'd piled on top of Mum's kitchen table and pretended that it was a car. The table couldn't take the weight of four girls and there was a loud creak as one of the legs buckled and snapped off. Mum went absolutely mental but Dad just laughed. By nature, my father was the much calmer of the two. On another occasion we decided to strip all the pillowcases off the pillows, push our legs inside, and use them as cloth sledges to race down the stairs. It wasn't long afterwards that Jon came up with a plan to try to control us; he decided he would try and frighten us half to death! He began by showing us horror movies but would always send Lucy, who was still only eight years old, to bed. With my younger sister safely tucked up, Ashley and Beca and I would watch *Hellraiser* or *Pet Cemetery*. However,

Jon was particularly cruel and refused to let us cover our faces even when the films became really scary. He was weird like that. One night, a few months later, Jon waited for Mum and Dad to leave for their planned night at the pub. He put on a film and invited his friend Simon over to watch it with us. Simon was tall and stocky and he wore these really strange tight jeans that were horrible. To little girls like us Simon had seemed really old, but in reality he was probably only in his mid-twenties, and he had light-brown hair that he combed into a severe parting. There was a barn further down along the country road, just minutes from our house. Simon would take us there, lift out his camera, and take lots of photographs. He'd ask us to strip down to our vest and pants. Sometimes he'd persuade us to take our vests off too. We were only young and he would make it sound exciting, like a game, so we had no idea what he was up to. He took more photographs of me in my bedroom. Even though I was still a kid, I knew something wasn't right but I didn't tell my parents because I didn't want to get into trouble. But the more he got away with stuff, the more twisted Jon became. Looking back, I'm sure he enjoyed our fear and the power he held over us. One evening he took us over to his house. He stood there – his eyes wide – and told us his kitchen was haunted by a poltergeist. Then he locked us all inside. Lucy was so scared that she couldn't stop crying. Afterwards, she hated it whenever Jon came over to babysit because she was frightened to death of him and what he might do. The next time he came over to ours, Lucy told him she had a headache. He was laughing because he'd locked Ashley in the front room and was standing in our hallway, holding onto the door handle. I pushed past to try and help, but he shoved me into the room with her. Beca tried to run out of the front door, but he held it closed – his foot wedged up against it – to stop her from leaving.

'I think I'm going to be sick,' I heard Lucy cry from the other side of the door.

Eventually, he let us out of the front room, but he'd already locked the front door so none of us could escape the house. Lucy became so terrified that she climbed out of the front-room window to escape. Jon spotted her through the glass and chased her down the garden path. I'm not sure if Lucy blabbed, but not long afterwards Mum told me Jon wouldn't be babysitting any more.

'Why?' I asked, wondering if she'd found out about the awful horror movies we'd watched.

But she refused to elaborate.

'He just won't!' she insisted, picking up a pair of oven gloves. Putting them on, she lifted a hot dish from the oven and rested it on the side of the worktop. 'Right, tea's ready, so go and get your sister, and don't forget to wash your hands!'

Mum didn't say anything else but she didn't have to. I realised the conversation about Jon was over. It wasn't until many years later I heard he'd gone on to babysit another family – a girl and two boys. The boys later complained to their parents that Jon had touched them inappropriately. They were horrified and immediately called the police, who raided Jon's house. With hindsight, it was clear Jon liked little boys but his pal Simon definitely had an unhealthy interest in young girls. Rumour had it the police also discovered a stash of porn at Jon's house and God only knows what at Simon's. I don't know what happened to them after that, but I never saw Jon again.

However, working for Barry, I'd already moved on. Although I wasn't even a teenager, I felt I'd grown up overnight and, in many ways, I had. Soon, Ashley and I were regularly running 'errands' for Barry. Mum didn't have a clue, of course, because I was careful how and where I would meet him. Sometimes I'd slip out of school and we would arrange to meet up near the top park. Barry would pick me up in his van and we'd go out into Wales on 'errands'. I knew he was a drug dealer and a clever one at that. Barry realised the police would never stop and search a vehicle with a child sitting in the passenger seat. Together, we'd cross county lines, delivering heroin, cocaine and weed to everyone and anyone who would pay him the right price. I never handled the money; I always left that to Barry.

Sometimes Ashley would travel with us; sometimes it would just be me and Barry. Unlike Jon, our old babysitter, I never found Barry creepy. However, around a year after I'd first started running drugs for him I saw something that freaked me out. His eldest step-daughter, Beca, had just turned thirteen and was a bit of a girly girl, who wore her long blonde hair down her back. We'd been sitting on the bed in Angela's bedroom, looking through drawers, searching for fags to steal, hide, and smoke in peace. Angela never opened any curtains, which didn't surprise me once I'd ventured inside. The house was always in total chaos; it was really messy with torn carpets, cig ends on the floor and clothes strewn everywhere. I wondered if she kept the curtains closed on purpose so that the neighbours couldn't see how she lived. If I'd thought it was messy downstairs then upstairs was a real doss house. Beca and I were sitting on the double bed when Barry came sauntering into the room, holding a fistful of cash. He was smiling like a Cheshire cat as he sat down on top of the bed and started to count his money, methodically laying it out across the top of the duvet. I knew it was money he'd just collected from our latest run. I looked on in fascination as he spread all the £10 and £20 notes out in a line until soon they'd covered the top half of the bed. Money made Barry happy, and today he seemed in a really good mood.

'Not bad, eh?' he said, giving me a wink.

Beca hadn't been paying much attention to the money or Barry so she was shocked when he lunged over and tried to grab her. At first, I wasn't sure if they were having a pretend fight but then Barry plunged his hand down the front of Beca's trousers and began to rub between her thighs. At first, she froze, but then I sensed her embarrassment. She wriggled and tried to move away from his grip, but Barry's hand followed her. Then they began to struggle as she tried to push her step-dad off, but Barry was determined and much stronger than she was. I felt absolutely mortified and didn't know what to say or do; instead, I sat there – rooted to the bed. Time seemed to move slowly as though the three of us were caught up in some kind of weird, warped dream. We were still sitting on the top of the duvet but Barry became rougher and forced his hand deeper, all the time grinning like a maniac. Somehow, my friend managed to free herself and push him away. I wasn't sure if Barry would go mad, but he suddenly began to laugh out loud as though it had all been a joke. He was still chuckling as he lay back on the bed and clasped his hands behind his head, as though he was on a day out at the beach. It sounds silly but, although I knew what he'd done had been wrong, even with the drug runs I was still a naive child and I wasn't aware that some men did that sort of thing to little girls. Still, I became much more wary of Barry following that day, even though he'd never touched me sexually. I continued to accompany him on drug runs because I thought it was fun and exciting, like an undercover spy in a film. However, what I didn't realise then was that Barry was grooming me. Sometimes he'd leave his van parked in the driveway and we'd venture out on a drug run in Angela's car – a battered, old, dark-blue estate. I don't know if she realised what he was up to or not, but he always stashed his drugs away in the washroom at home, so she must have stumbled across them at some point. At least whenever we used Angela's car it meant we'd all get a seat. It was better than me or Ashley having to slum it with the rubbish in the back of the van. We'd usually start off at Fat Bryn's house, then deliver to various flats and houses across the country-side – whoever had put in an order with Barry that day. He always did the talking, especially at Bryn's house. Ashley and I would sit on the sofa, smoking or drinking alcopops – usually Smirnoff Ice or VK – the blue one was always my favourite. Bryn used to laugh; I think it tickled him to see two little girls, sitting on his couch, knocking back the booze, swearing like fishwives and smoking like chimneys.

One day, ages after the incident with Beca in the bedroom, I'd bunked off from school so that I could meet Barry and do a run. It had reached a point where I would just get up and leave during the middle of a lesson. I had become confident – cocky – and I felt I had so much more important things to do with my life than sit and rot in a classroom. I thought I knew it all, even though I was still a little girl. That day, I left the classroom and kept on walk-ing; I didn't even look back, not even after the teacher had called my name.

Barry was waiting for me, parked up near the school in his white van.

'Get in,' he said, leaning over the passenger seat to open the door. I climbed into the passenger seat, grabbed the seatbelt and fastened it around me. The black belt dragged against my school uniform, which crumpled beneath.

'Want one?' Barry asked, popping the metal lid off a tin of roll-ups he'd made earlier. He rattled the tin impatiently, waiting for me to take one. I was surprised; I hadn't even asked him for one. I wondered why he was being so nice. He'd always been chatty but today he seemed to be in an extra good mood.

We both sat there smoking inside his van as he turned the key, started up the van, and the engine fired into life. The whole vehicle shuddered as he let go of the handbrake and we began to roll forwards, trundling along the narrow road. I looked out of the window and was in the middle of a daydream when I felt a hot weight in the centre of my lap. I glanced down and spotted Barry's hand resting there; I watched as it moved from the top of my skirt, underneath the fabric, before tracing along my leg and up towards the inside of my thigh. His hot fingers gripped at my flesh as his hand snaked higher and higher. My face flushed with embarrassment and I squirmed in my seat, hoping it might be enough to free me, but Barry held on. Fear snagged at the back of my throat, stealing my breath away as I began to panic. I knew I couldn't ask Barry to remove his hand because I thought he might be angry with me. Instead, I tried to focus on the road ahead, hoping and praying he would release me soon. His hand remained there for what felt like an eternity but was probably only a couple of minutes, and then he let go. He didn't say a word or even try to explain what he'd just done. Instead, he just laughed and shrugged his shoulders as though it had all been a joke.

Had I got it wrong? Had I imagined it? My mind whirred as I began to question myself, even though I knew what he'd done, and so did Barry. We didn't speak; instead, I turned away from him and stared out of the window. I felt confused because I didn't know what it meant. I'd seen him do something similar to Beca.

Did it mean he loved me as much as his daughter?

But I didn't ask because I didn't feel that I could. With his hands now back on the steering wheel, I breathed a sigh of relief and pushed it to the back of my mind. I had a brand new, exciting life and I didn't want it to end.

Not long afterwards, I'd decided that I'd outgrown school. It had reached a point where I no longer cared about it or myself. Instead, I would simply stand up, grab my bag and leave.

'Emily Vaughn, sit down, now!' the teacher warned as I turned to leave. But she didn't frighten me – no one did. I was mixing with drug dealers and junkies now, so teachers held no fear.

I grabbed my bag, pulled it onto my shoulder, and headed towards the door. A sea of eyes in the classroom followed me as I did.

'Where on earth do you think you're going?' she continued, but I was already halfway through the door.

I'd decided school had nothing to teach me; nothing at all.

'I don't need this,' I mumbled as the door slammed behind me. 'You can all just fuck off!' I hollered.

With Barry on my side, I felt untouchable. Fired up by a new-found confidence, I thought I ruled the world; by now I was twelve years old, and Barry had shown me life didn't have to be boring. Not only that; I knew I'd learn more outside the classroom than in it. Of course, the headmaster went mad and would regularly ring Mum to tell her what I'd done. After answering his calls, she'd be frantic – outside, scouring the streets, looking for me. Once she even managed to catch me; I was hiding behind a tree when she grabbed me. She was so angry that she dragged me all the way back to the school kicking and screaming.

'I don't know what's got into you lately! I'm not having this!' she scolded, as she pulled me into reception and asked to speak to the headmaster.

Afterwards, I became more careful; I knew I couldn't let her catch me with Barry. If I spotted her on the street I'd ask him to park up somewhere out of sight so that I could jump down from the van. Then I'd casually stroll past her and lie when she asked where I'd been.

'I've been walking around the estate.'

But I knew she didn't believe me.

One afternoon Barry and I were distracted, chatting about something. The radio was blaring away as we drove back onto the estate. Mum saw us before we'd seen her. My heart was hammering inside my chest as Barry pulled up alongside the kerb and wound down his window.

'I've been looking all over for you!' Mum began, staring over at Barry. I could see she was just about to ask him what I was doing in his van, when he piped up.

'Hiya, I found her wandering around the estate so I picked her up. I was just bringing her home. I hope that's okay?'

Mum went to say something but stopped herself. Barry gestured to the road with his hand.

'I was just driving her back to yours now.'

I could tell she was a bit stumped.

'Oh right. Well, thanks, Barry. That's very kind of you, but I'll take her from here. I've been out everywhere looking for you!' she said, turning her attention towards me. I realised then that Barry was so quick that he was almost invincible.

'What the hell has got into you?' Mum continued to scold as she dragged me out of the van. 'I don't know what's going on but you are going straight back to school!'

I knew I'd never win the argument so I let her take me back, only to do the same thing over and over again. When I wasn't playing truant from school I'd be in the classroom, delivering drugs to other kids. Barry sold to a lot of their parents but he would pass the drugs through Beca and me to their children. By now, he had begun to take more and more risks, using us as his fail-safe cover. There was one lad at school, called Lewis, who Beca sold dope to, and another boy, Michael, whose dad would put in a weekly order for weed, passed on behalf of Barry through me. I didn't care if I got caught with drugs at school – I didn't care about much any more because I was out of control and didn't want to be there. Word got around and soon the other kids knew that if they wanted drugs they needed to come to me.

One day, about a year after I'd started secondary school, I got into a fight with a younger boy on my estate called Donovan. His mother had been dating another local drug dealer, who found out I'd been delivering drugs for Barry. Donovan and I had a bit of a tussle in the street and his mum called the police. However, before they'd arrived, Donovan punched me so hard in the face that he gave me a black eye. Another adult from the estate – a passer-by – saw what had happened and tried to intervene. However, by the time the police arrived it was me, not him, who was charged with assault and battery. The passer-by, who had tried to hold me and Donovan apart, was also charged even though they'd hardly touched him. But Donovan had a slight bruise to the side of his face and, it seemed, that had been enough evidence to charge me. I was summoned to attend an adult court to answer the charges. The hearing was adjourned and I was bailed, but then my school found out and I was eventually expelled. I was ordered to see a counsellor to help deal with my 'anger management'. The court case was eventually dropped against the adult, who had only ever tried to help, but, because it had been heard in an adult court, I was given a criminal record. I wasn't even a teenager but I felt as though my life was over; I'd been labelled a troublemaker and it was a label I would spend the rest of my life trying to shake off.

Of course, Mum was furious and bitterly disappointed in me. She was also clueless and completely baffled by the gradual change in my behaviour. But, above all, she was bloody angry.

'You're not sitting around here all day; if you can't go to school then we will have to bring school to you,' she decided.

'Eh?'

She had it all worked out. She contacted Len – a retired male teacher – who lived further down the road. Len was already home-schooling five children on the estate and soon he was home-schooling me. It was torture, sitting there alongside the other kids, trying to learn maths and English. Unlike me, the other children were real swots, and they loved nothing more than revising, reading and working hard. I felt like a square peg in a round hole.

I still saw Barry occasionally but by now Mum was keeping a close eye on me; she'd even take me to Len's lessons herself, sit down and bring me home again. There was no escape. Thankfully, I only had two days of learning each week, so the rest of the time was pretty much my own to fill. Obviously, I was supposed to be working, but homework was the furthest thing from my mind.

There was another man called Tony, who used to drive his van onto our estate to rent out DVDs to householders. I knew that his DVD rental business was a cover story for selling drugs. He was friends with my mate's dad. Tony was from the roughest housing estate for miles; he was also friends with Barry, and soon I began 'working' for both of them even though they were in direct competition against each other. I wondered if Barry might get annoyed with me, but he never did; as long as he could rely on me for our 'drug runs' then he was happy. Working with Tony was different to what I'd been used to with Barry. Instead of just delivering or collecting a DVD from a house, I would deliver drugs and collect money.

'Take this to number three, and then this to number twelve,' Tony instructed, pressing a couple of wrapped packets of drugs into the palm of my hand before pulling a couple of DVDs off the shelf.

I nodded; I knew what I had to do. By now I was skilled at hiding drugs, although my once baggy children's T-shirts had now been replaced by trendy crop tops. But it didn't matter – I knew exactly where to put the drugs so they didn't show or, more importantly, fall out. Whenever someone answered the door they would hand me the money to take back to Tony and I would give them their drugs and 'cover' DVD. To the outside world it looked completely legitimate; I was simply helping Tony out with his DVD rental firm. But the reality was I was still drug running.

'Here you go,' I said, placing some notes inside Tony's hand once I was sitting safely within the confines of his van. 'That's from number twelve and this,' I said, digging a £20 note from the back pocket of my jeans, 'is from number three.'

Tony nodded and grinned; his open mouth revealed a revolting row of small, childlike yellowed teeth that made him look a bit like a rat.

'Good girl. Same again next week?'

'Yep,' I agreed, blowing cigarette smoke out of the corner of my mouth.

I took another long, deep drag and wondered how I'd come so far in such a short time. Tony would give me free DVDs for my trouble or the odd £5 note to spend, but that was it; I'd effectively carved out my own little niche as the local drugs runner.

When I wasn't with Tony, or being home-schooled by Len, with Mum breathing down my neck, I was meeting up with Barry.

'I'm just off to the shop,' I called out one afternoon as I pulled on my jacket and headed for the front door.

'Wait!' Mum shouted from the kitchen, but it was too late, I'd already left. Once I was outside, I would be gone for hours.

I didn't have a mobile phone back then, but I didn't need one. Barry lived opposite and, whenever he needed me, he would whistle for me like a dog. Sometimes he'd even call out his dog's name which was also my cue. Sometimes Ashley would call or whistle me over. During quick, snatched conversations we'd arrange to meet at the top of the estate, far away from prying eyes. By now, Ashley had also stopped going to school, so the three of us would go off in the van, crossing county lines to deliver more drugs. We would hide cocaine, heroin and weed, whatever people had ordered, inside our crop tops and walk the streets as though we were two innocent little girls playing outside.

One day, Barry had parked the van up outside a house I'd never been to before. The property seemed dark and damp and we had to climb quite a few steps to reach the back door. There were two men and half a dozen teenage boys sitting, smoking and chatting on the sofa. I guessed they couldn't have been much more than fifteen years old yet, here they were, smoking drugs in the middle of the afternoon in a nondescript rundown house in the Welsh countryside.

The two men were much older – both middle-aged – around the same age as Barry.

'Here,' one of the men said as soon as I'd walked in through the back door, 'do you know how to rinse coke?'

I shook my head; I was twelve years old – I didn't have a clue what 'rinse' meant.

'Come here and I'll show you,' he said, beckoning his hand for me to follow. 'You'll learn more from me in the next five minutes than you'll ever learn in school,' he said, looking over at Barry knowingly.

'Go on then,' Barry nodded and pushed me towards the man.

Then he turned and headed over to the front room to sort out his drug deal. I realised it must have been a big deal because Barry hadn't used me to deliver it, but had come inside himself.

I did as I was told and followed the man into the kitchen, which was large, dark and scruffy. It looked like a squat, and all the windows had been blacked out using rags instead of curtains. The kitchen had a cooker and sink – all the usual stuff – but everything was covered in a thin coat of grime. There were a few men sitting at a round table in the centre of the room. They looked up curiously as I entered the room but, other than that, they didn't pay me much attention. They were sitting on wooden chairs but they were all scratched and scuffed up against a filthy blue lino floor. On top of the table was a various array of weights and knives to sort, divide and weigh out drugs. The room smelled strongly of petrol, as though someone had been running a car engine inside it. The smell was acrid; it made my eyes smart and it clung at the back of my throat, making me choke.

'You okay?' the man turned to ask. Both my eyes were streaming; big, fat tears ran down both cheeks. I rubbed them away defiantly with the back of my sleeve and nodded. 'Good. Now, grab that pan, will you?' he said, pointing at a small, deep saucepan.

He took it from me and placed it on top of the stove. Then he poured in a jug of water and, in a separate bowl, mixed cocaine with some other white powder. The gas was turned high to try and boil the water before he lowered the bowl with the powder and cocaine down into it. Slowly but surely, the water started to boil, causing the coke to crystal-lise inside the bowl. I watched totally mesmerised as it began to turn like glue before my very eyes. I glanced inside and estimated that there must have been about 40 grams which – at between £70 and £80 a gram – was worth around £3,000. I glanced up at the man. He was middle-aged – in his forties – and tall, with black hair and a cap. Like an expert, he continued to watch and wait as the cocaine turned to goo and the room began to fill with the strange aroma of cat piss.

'Here, pass me that paperclip,' he said suddenly, waving his fingers.

I picked one up from the kitchen work surface.

'This?'

The man nodded as the water in the pan continued to boil, leaving a sticky clear mixture in the bowl. He took the paperclip and stirred the gluey substance a few more times with the paperclip. The mixture seemed to harden as he plucked a bit up with the metal clip. Then he pulled it up and out, like clear toffee. The small dollops were placed on a baking sheet on the side, waiting to cool into individual 'rocks'. These would be later bagged up and sold as crack cocaine. I was still watching, totally hypnotised, when he noticed.

'Here,' he said, handing me the paperclip, 'you wanna to have a go at washing this coke?'

I nodded, even though my heart was beating twice as fast inside my chest; I was absolutely terrified I'd mess it up.

'That's right,' he encouraged, expertly guiding my hand and the paperclip to try and 'collect' enough crystals to form a rock. 'No, not too much!'

I felt my face flush bright red because I didn't want to let Barry down. I dropped a bit back down into the bowl and looked up to him for confirmation.

'Yeah, that's better; that's it.'

Moments later, he called through to Barry in the front room.

'Yep.'

'She's good, this one; she's really got the hang of it!'

I heard Barry laugh, followed by the men sitting at the kitchen table. But I didn't care because I knew I'd done well; inside I felt secretly proud. I continued to stand at the cooker separating the crack so that it could be bagged up into individual batches. It looked a bit like crumbly fudge – the type grandparents would buy from old-fashioned sweet shops. My hands were small and nimble, which meant I'd soon made light work of what had been an easy but fiddly task. It was a whole new world to me; one even darker than the last. But, to the men, 'rinsing' or 'washing' coke was as normal and everyday as making a Sunday roast.

'Good girl,' the stranger said, patting my back fondly.

I grinned, relieved I'd proved myself, done well for Barry and not shown myself up. The man's eyes were still wide as we watched the rest of the batch cook and I realised he was right; I'd learned more today, standing in that grotty kitchen, than I'd ever learnt inside a classroom.

CHAPTER THREE

THE WARDROBE

By now I had no interest in hanging around with kids of my own age; they all seemed childish and pathetic. I was mixing with the adults and it made me feel special – more grown-up, somehow. But there were times when I felt a little out of my depth. By now I was sneaking off to help Barry three or four times a week. Like Tony, he'd give me the odd £5 note or a ten pack of Lambert & Butler fags for my trouble.

One afternoon, when I didn't have any home schooling, I sneaked out of the house to go off with Barry. We had pulled up outside Fat Bryn's house. Bryn had two teenage sons; they were nothing like him because they were both skinny. They must have only been fifteen and sixteen years old, and were called Michael and Stuart. Unbelievably, Bryn also had a wife called Samantha but I very rarely saw her. I wondered how she could bear to be married to someone as repulsive as Bryn. Unlike Samantha, Michael and Stuart were usually in whenever Barry and I called round. Bryn and his boys kept an axe by the fireside; I presumed it was used to chop wood. This particular afternoon, Bryn and Barry had a bit of an argument – nothing serious – just a bit of a disagreement. I was sitting smoking a fag on the sofa when Barry suddenly jumped up, grabbed the axe from the heart and began waving it around as though he was an extra from a horror film.

'Fuck's sake, Barry, sit down!' Bryn huffed, trying to defuse the situation. But Barry was having none of it.

'Sit down? Sit down, you fat fucker! I'll give you sit down,' he said, waving the edge of the axe near Bryn's wobbly turkey neck as though he would behead him. He got so close that Bryn swerved backwards on the sofa.

Bryn's sons seemed as terrified as their father. I freaked out too, but kept my mouth shut. I didn't have the nerve to speak up. Instead, I was sitting there, watching, and waiting to see what Barry would do next.

'Stop trying to rob me, you fat fucker! You owe me, and you know you do. Just pay me my money, like you said you would, and I'll put this down,' Barry threatened.

The edge of the metal glinted in the dim light and I wondered how sharp it really was and if he could cut Bryn open with it.

Swish!

The axe made a whistling noise as it sliced through the air next to Bryn's head, causing him to duck down.

'Whoa, Barry!' he cried as his boys looked on, petrified.

'Pay me what you owe me, otherwise you'll get it,' Barry warned, jumping on top of the coffee table.

Bryn put his arms out to try and defend himself.

Swish!

The axe passed so close by that I had to double check he hadn't just opened up Bryn's fleshy hands.

'Fucking hell, Barry! Calm down!' Bryn gasped.

But Barry refused to stop.

Swish! Swish!

Fear rose like vomit at the back of my throat and I swallowed hard to try and push it back down. The atmosphere in the room had grown so tense that you could almost touch it.

Swish!

'Okay, okay!' Bryn said, holding up his hand. He plunged the other deep into the pocket of his jogger bottoms and pulled out a battered black wallet.

'Another £20. There, there!' he said peeling it away from a wad of notes and slapping it down on the table at Barry's feet.

Satisfied he'd won, Barry jumped down, scooped up the note and pushed it inside his shirt pocket. Then he calmly walked over to the hearth and propped the axe up against the fireplace. My eyes darted over to Bryn's boys, who were still wide-eyed and terrified. We'd all expected a bloodbath, but Barry had made his point, got his money, and now he was satisfied. Neither the axe nor the threat was ever spoken of. But after that day Bryn never short-changed Barry again.

If I'd felt out of my depth with Bryn and the axe, then it was nothing compared to Liam, who was another babysitter my parents had drafted in. With a stocky build and a thick mop of blond boyband hair, Liam was good-looking and in his early twenties. I had a crush on him as soon as he called at the door.

'Thanks, Liam. There's food in the fridge, if you're hungry. I've fed the girls, so put them to bed about nine, and watch some telly. We shouldn't be too late back,' Mum said chirpily as they headed out for the evening.

I hadn't been that thrilled when Mum had first mentioned she'd got us a new babysitter, but when I found out it was Liam, I was delighted I was still only twelve, but Liam would become my first real crush. So, when he climbed into bed with me later that night to 'chat' I was over the moon. But soon the chatting progressed to him putting his hands inside my clothes. We would kiss too – like boyfriend and girlfriend – and I convinced myself that this was exactly what we were and it was the real deal.

The following day, I pulled my sister Lucy to one side. I was bursting with happiness and desperate to tell someone – anyone – about what had happened.

'You know Liam?' I whispered. 'He's my boyfriend!'

Lucy's eyes widened with shock.

'But he's old! He's like twenty or something!'

I giggled.

'I know, but he loves me and I love him!'

She was surprised, but I didn't care. Lucy was only ten and she didn't know about life like I did. I was all grown-up. My thirteenth birthday was fast approaching and I thought I knew it all.

Liam would even show us porn on the TV. He'd send Lucy to bed and get frisky with me. One night he pulled me into bed. I was worried because Lucy had a twin bed and she was asleep only feet away on the other side of the room.

'Look at it,' he said, forcing my head under the covers to look at his erection. I didn't really want to but I told myself this was what boyfriends and girlfriends must do.

'That's it; now touch it, Em.'

But I didn't want to touch it; the situation had grown out of control so quickly that I felt as though I was drowning.

'Come on, touch it; I won't bite,' he whispered before shifting himself on top of me.

That's when he tried to have sex with me. I lay there – half scared to death – staring up at the *X-Files* posters on my bedroom wall. I wondered how I'd got myself into this – a situation far more grown-up than I was. It felt awkward; I became so upset and confused that I began to cry.

'Stop it!' he hissed as he tried to continue. But, try as he might, he couldn't do it. Angry and frustrated, he grabbed my hand and pulled me up from my bed.

He dragged me through to the bathroom and that's when I spotted it – a small trickle of blood dribbling down from between my legs. I was bleeding. He'd done that to me.

'It hurts,' I winced. I became so distraught that I started to cry.

'Shush!' Liam snapped, grabbing Mum's flannel off the side. 'Here, wipe yourself.'

Afterwards, even though Liam had rinsed and dried off the flannel we could still see a trace of blood. He grabbed it, stuffed it inside his bag, and took it home with him so Mum wouldn't find out. He also made me promise not to tell.

'I won't.'

Sometimes, Liam's friend David would come over and watch porn at ours whenever Mum and Dad were out. I told myself that's what boyfriends and girlfriends must do. But one day Liam stopped coming around altogether.

'Where's Liam? Why doesn't he babysit any more?' I asked Mum, but she wouldn't answer and refused to make eye contact with me.

I never found out what happened to Liam, and his sudden disappearance broke my heart. I thought we'd been a couple but the reality was Liam had been a paedophile. I later heard he'd had a bit of a breakdown and had left the estate. I never saw him again.

I was still helping Barry out but someone must have tipped off the police – either that or they were watching him – because soon his house was being raided all the time.

'I don't want you calling over to see Ashley or Beca any more,' Mum told me one day.

'But they're my friends! Why can't I see them?'

But she refused to budge. She insisted that, while she didn't mind me playing outside in the street with them, she didn't want me going inside the house.

'But Angela's your friend, and you still see her!'

'That's different.'

'Why?' I demanded.

Mum pursed her lips together as though she wanted to say something but couldn't.

'Yes, but I'm an adult. Listen, I don't want to talk about it any more; I just don't want you going inside their house, all right?'

But it wasn't.

A week or so later, Barry whistled over the fence and beckoned me over.

'Hi, Em, I've not seen you lately. Things okay at home?'

I couldn't tell him Mum had banned me from calling at their house, but I wasn't sure what to say. Instead, I scuffed the bottom of my shoe against the side of the kerb, avoiding eye contact in case he could tell I was lying.

'Suppose so.'

Barry nodded.

'Good, good. Listen, Em, I need you to do something for me.'

I looked up, a little intrigued.

'What?'

Barry checked over each shoulder that no one was listening to our conversation.

'I need you to hide something for me; it's the bastard police, Em. They're trying to stitch me up. I need you to look after something for me – not for long,' he insisted, 'just for a little while – until they get bored with me and pick on someone else.'

'Right,' I mumbled. I didn't need to ask what it was.

'So, is that a yes?' Barry said, dipping down, trying to catch my eye.

'Hmm?'

'Good. Listen, meet me around the back in five minutes and I'll give it to you, but, Em …' he paused and held a finger up against his lips. 'Not a word; not to anyone, okay? This is just between me and you because … well, we go back a long way, don't we?'

I'd never been a friend of Barry because he didn't have friends, only enemies. But I was also smart enough not to say no. I couldn't afford to make an enemy of the local drug dealer.

'No problem.'

I hung around the back of his house so that Mum wouldn't see me. Moments later he reappeared holding what looked like an ice-cream tub in his hands. But instead of smooth vanilla ice cream, the container was filled to the brim with 'bricks' of heroin that he'd tightly wrapped in black polythene. I took the tub and pushed it up inside my hoodie.

'Good girl, Em,' Barry nodded. 'Now hide it somewhere where your mum and dad won't find it. Keep it away from Lucy, too. I've got a lot riding on this; you can't fuck this up; I trust you.'

'I won't,' I promised, and I meant it.

With the tub of drugs inside my top, I sneaked around the back of our house and opened the door. I stopped in my tracks and listened out for Mum, but the house seemed quiet; I knew Dad would be at work and Lucy at school. I shared a bedroom with my sister so I knew it would have to be well hidden. I stood in the middle of the room, my eyes scanning it to try and decide where the best place would be. There were books and DVDs lined up on one shelf and a desk, holding a portable TV, stereo and speakers underneath. There wasn't a single empty space on the walls, which I'd plastered with film posters, including Johnny Depp. My cute childhood bear wallpaper had also been covered with cuttings from teenage magazines and brightly coloured pop posters because I was obsessed with the Spice Girls. The room was cluttered with stuff. Lucy's bed was on the opposite side of the room. I got down on my knees, pulled up the edge of my duvet and checked underneath the bed. It was pretty untidy even though Mum always pulled things out whenever she hoovered up to clean the carpet; I couldn't risk it. How would I even begin to explain a stash of heroin worth hundreds of pounds inside an ice-cream tub underneath my bed?

No, I decided, I had to find somewhere safe. And that's when I spotted it – my dark blue wardrobe against the wall. I'd covered it with photographs of me, Lucy, Ashley and Beca. There was also an anti-bullying poster, and a sticker that read 'Rehab is for quitters'.

'The wardrobe, that's it!'

The top of the wardrobe was lined with different coloured bottles and knick-knacks I'd collected over the years. I pulled open the doors and glanced down. The bottom of it was buried with old shoes and games balanced on top of each other. I considered shifting them but then I looked up. There was a shelf at the top crammed with stuffed toys and teddies. I took a few out and realised that if I pushed the ice-cream tub right to the back of it I'd be able to cover the front with toys. The teddies were there because I felt too old to have them in my bedroom, but too young to want to part with them. I also knew that no one ever moved them – it was the perfect hiding place. Within minutes I'd rearranged them, pushing the heroin deep behind stuffed dogs, cats, rabbits, teddies and Disney characters. I stood back to admire my handiwork.

Perfect. No one would ever guess what they were hiding.

I'd been guarding Barry's heroin for three days when early one morning I heard the sound of sirens. A sea of blue lights filled my bedroom, flashing against the wall as a squad of police cars screeched up outside. They were raiding Barry's house along with another half a dozen others on the estate. Curtains twitched as other neighbours looked on; I stared through my bedroom window – the drugs hidden just feet away to the left of me, but I didn't feel frightened. I knew they were safe with me. Outside was bathed in a sea of blue, flashing lights. Dozens of parked squad cars illuminated different rooftops in adjoining streets as the multiple raids took place. There was even a helicopter circling up above the estate. I spotted Ashley; she was hanging out of her bedroom window, watching the drama unfold on the streets below. Then I saw Angela answer the front door, as police slipped around the back of the house to stop Barry escaping through the back door. A group of officers with sniffer dogs bundled inside the property, searching for Barry's drugs.

'You all right, Ashley?' I called loudly across the street and over to my friend.

'Yeah, you?'

I nodded.

'Police are raiding us again, Em. You think they'd have better things to do; there's nothing here,' she said pointedly.

The officer who was guarding the front door looked up at her and then me.

I counted around a dozen officers going inside Barry's house, but I knew they wouldn't find a thing because he was always one step ahead of everyone, or so I thought.

The raid on Angela's house had been the biggest yet and soon tongues had started to wag across the estate. People began to say things about Barry that they'd previously been far too frightened to voice out loud. A few days later, Barry told me it was safe to return the ice-cream tub, so I did. I pushed it underneath my hoodie and carried it around the back of his house, whistling over to him to come and take it back from me.

'Thanks, Em, I owe you.' He winked.

I felt my stomach turn; I couldn't explain it; I just felt unsettled by it.

A short time later I heard Mum telling my dad that Angela and Barry had split up.

'I don't know what happened. They say she's thrown him out and I don't blame her. Think she'd had enough. They reckon he's been dealing drugs,' Mum said, her voice floating out from the kitchen into the hallway, where I sat listening on the stairs.

'A plumber, my arse,' I heard Dad scoff.

I shuddered; if only they knew.

Not long afterwards, Barry had disappeared altogether, just as Liam had done. I wondered if it was something to do with me – people came, grew close to me, and then left.

I didn't have a clue where Barry had gone but I felt sad that our drug runs had finally come to an end. I still had Tony, of course, but I'd loved going out with Barry because it had made me feel valued and wanted. However, the constant raids on his house made me realise just how close to the wind I'd been sailing. In many ways, now he'd gone I was free to start all over again.

CHAPTER FOUR

THE SWIMMING POOL

By the time I'd turned fourteen I was told I'd no longer have to do home-schooling. I was both relieved and delighted. Instead, Mum told me the local authority would be enrolling me on a childcare course – something I'd always wanted to do. I couldn't wait to start at my local technical college – a big 1960s steel and fibreglass board building – situated in the centre of town, not far from the seafront. Even though most people went there to undertake vocational courses after leaving school, the local authority allowed me to start a few years earlier, and I joined in autumn 2000 – a few months before my fifteenth birthday.

The first person I met was a girl called Andrea, who was tasked with giving me a tour of the place.

'This is where we have our lessons, and down there,' she said, pointing along the corridor behind me, 'is where the toilets are. Any questions?'

I shook my head. The older girl was really skinny with long, thin, mousy hair. She was quite plain looking but she seemed approachable enough; I knew she was eighteen, several years older than me. I felt a little unsure so I racked my brains, trying to think of a question that wouldn't make me sound like a muppet.

'And where do we go if we, you know, need a fag?'

'You smoke?' she replied, a little surprised.

'Course I do!'

'Ahh, I can see that we are gonna get on, even though I don't! Come on, follow me, I'll show you.'

By the time my first day had arrived, the only person I recognised was Andrea. Thankfully, we were paired together because she was in all my lessons. From that day on, she became my best friend, even though she was a whole school year older than me. Although she was skeletal with no breasts and a figure that seemed to be straight up and down, Andrea seemed to have a constant stream of attention from the college boys.

A week or so after I'd started, I was standing outside smoking a fag when I offered Andrea one.

'Go on,' I said, waving the fag packet at her. 'Take one.'

'I don't really …'

'Oh go on, one won't kill you!'

In truth, I was just trying to fit in. My worst fear was to be an outsider with no friends. I was sick of feeling like the odd one out; all I wanted to do now was be accepted. So, whenever someone went for a fag, I'd join them. Likewise, if anyone brought in a bottle of vodka, I'd be the first one to take a swig of it.

One day, Andrea and I were standing outside college when a tall, reed-thin lad passed by. The boy noticed her and lifted his hand to wave.

'Do you know him?' I asked, looking round at her.

Andrea blushed.

'Yeah,' she replied coyly, turning away with a smile on her face.

'How? How do you know him? Go on, tell me!'

She turned back to face me and that's when I noticed she'd gone even more red.

'I had sex with him.'

My mouth fell wide open. I'd never heard anyone talk so openly about sex before.

I was just thinking what to say when another ginger-haired boy passed.

'I've had him, too.' She smirked, bursting out laughing.

'You haven't!'

'I have; and I'll tell you something for nothing – he was much better than the other one.'

Andrea winked and gave me a nudge with her elbow.

I was so shocked that I began to cough and then choke on my cigarette smoke. I'd been a drug runner for Barry but, apart from that, I was still totally naive about sex. Of course, Liam had tried it on with me, but we'd never had proper sex.

'So, how many lads have you slept with, Em?' she asked.

I glanced down at my feet and, although I tried my best, I felt the heat rise in my own cheeks.

'Come on, tell me? How many?'

I shook my head, not knowing quite what to say.

My friend leant forward and looked up at my face, which I'd tried to hide behind my long hair. I felt her eyes burning into me.

'Well? Come on, don't be shy!'

I shook my head.

'It's not that …' I stammered.

'Don't tell me you can't remember. God!' she said, cackling away to herself. 'And I thought I was bad …'

I remained silent as Andrea took another drag of her cigarette. She thought for a moment and then blew the smoke out of the side of her mouth sharply.

'What! Don't tell me! You're not a virgin, are you?'

My face grew even hotter and I refused to look at her as she screeched with laughter.

'No …' I said defensively. I didn't want my new friend to think I was a complete gimp.

'Oh, that's okay then. I couldn't be seen knocking about with a virgin. I've got my reputation to think of.'

I cringed inside. Thankfully, another one of our classmates – a girl called Carys – came over to join us.

'What you two talking about?' she asked, flicking on the lighter and holding the end of her cigarette in the flame.

'Men,' Andrea replied before I could.

'Oh those!' Carys laughed, using her fingertip to brush a stray strand of tobacco from her bottom lip. 'They're nothing but trouble.'

Thankfully, the conversation soon moved swiftly on.

''Ere,' Carys said, looking over both shoulders, 'you two heard about Michelle?'

We shook our heads.

Carys leaned in conspiratorially, so we did the same until soon we were huddled in a small group, like some sort of secret society.

'Okay, now, I didn't tell you this but you know she's pregnant, don't you?'

I gasped. Michelle was only fourteen, like me, but her baby face made her look even younger. She was a nice girl even though she was a bit rough around the edges.

'It's true,' Carys said, relishing in the drama of it all. 'And you know who the father is, don't you?'

She waited to build up the tension so that she could watch the surprise on both our faces when she dropped the bombshell answer.

'Paul.'

Andrea gasped and almost dropped her cigarette in the process.

'Not Paul, the one on that building course? Him in the year above?'

Carys nodded.

'Yes, the very same one.'

'But he's like … he's …'

'Eighteen, almost nineteen. Yep, I know. Fucking disgusting, isn't it? She's only a kid. There's a name for blokes like him.'

Liam the babysitter flashed through my mind and I shuddered.

'You okay, Em?'

It was Carys; she was staring at me.

'Yeah, I'm fine. I'm just a bit shocked, that's all.'

Carys inhaled some cigarette smoke and then blew it out through both nostrils. It poured from her nose like two long, grey, smoky fingers.

'You're telling me; I couldn't believe it when she told me in the toilets. I was so shocked. I said to her, "So, are you gonna keep it then?"'

'And what did she say?' Andrea interrupted. It was clear she was on tenterhooks, waiting to hear the rest of the gossip.

'She said she wasn't sure.'

Andrea shook her head, followed by Carys.

'Daft bitch! If that was me, I'd get rid of it sharpish. You wouldn't want a kid tying you down for ever now, would you?'

I shook my head too, even though I was still so shocked that I didn't know what to think.

A few days later Andrea asked me if I wanted to hang around at her house after college. I was so delighted to have a new best friend that I jumped at the chance.

'What shall we do?' I asked, as we pushed our textbooks into our bags after the last lesson had finished.

'I dunno; shall we go down the prom later?'

The promenade was a place where bored teenagers congregated during the winter months, long after the tourists had packed up at the end of the summer season and gone home.

'Yeah, that would be great!'

Although we were still neighbours and would still bump into each other occasionally, with Barry off the scene Ashley had all but disappeared from my life for the time being. So it felt good to have another friend in Andrea.

After we'd packed our bags, we walked back to her house and hung around for a bit. There wasn't much to do, so she suggested we go to see another girl called Ruth who lived nearby. Ruth lived with her dad, but we'd recently started hanging around together at a local takeaway shop. Someone suggested we should go over there to pick up burgers and chips. I'd never really noticed before but that evening Andrea had seemed really friendly with the men who worked behind the counter.

'Here, I'm bored now,' she announced suddenly after we'd finished eating our food. 'Let's go to the prom and hang out – see who's there.'

I grinned. That's what I loved about Andrea: she was always full of such good ideas.

It was a winter's evening, so the walk down to the promenade was dark and blustery as we neared the seafront. I pulled the sleeves of my thin sweatshirt over my hands and shivered as I scrunched it inside my fingers to try and anchor it down. It was absolutely Baltic! The path seemed uneven, and I glanced down at my feet and cursed; my black boots had platform heels that made me look much taller, but also made walking so much more treacherous.

'Whoa! You okay?' Andrea asked, laughing as my foot twisted awkwardly beneath me and I went over on my ankle.

'Yeah,' I said, also laughing. 'Bloody stupid boots!'

I was so desperate to impress her that I was determined nothing would ruin this for me – nothing.

We walked past the cemetery. Normally, walking near all the dead in their graves would have freaked me out but I was with Andrea, so I felt safe. I linked my arm through hers as we grew closer to the seafront. I'd expected to see groups of teenagers, other people to talk to or hang out with, but the place was completely deserted. It was quiet, apart from the roar of the black sea. The wind whistled along the prom; it carried pieces of chipped white enamel paint from ornamental wrought-iron railings away as sharp splinters in the breeze. I wrapped my arms around myself to try and keep warm as cold air whipped against me.

'What shall we do?' I asked, turning to Andrea as my eyes scoured the rest of the prom.

There wasn't a soul in sight. The ice-cream hut was all shuttered up, and even the toilets, usually crammed with desperate toddlers and fraught young mums during the height of summer, had been padlocked. The outside swimming pool had been drained, apart from a few muddy puddles of rainwater that had collected at the bottom. Even the crazy golf course – usually a wall of noise during tourist season – was deathly still. The whole place looked and felt like a ghost town.

'Oh, let's hang around a little bit longer,' Andrea suggested. Her rats'-tail hair blew straight in the breeze as she held a hand against the wind to try and light a cigarette. She'd quickly become a real hardcore smoker. 'Want one?' she asked, handing over the fag she'd just lit.

I took it to pass the time, but mainly to keep warm. Any warmth, even the sparse embers of a cigarette, felt better than nothing. The cigarette glowed brightly in my mouth as I took a drag. I glanced around again and felt a bit out of place. I didn't know why Andrea wanted to hang around when there was no one else there.

'Shall we go and sit in the shelter?' I suggested, pointing over to it.

But she seemed distracted.

'Hmm, in a minute,' Andrea mumbled, staring off into the distance.

I continued to smoke the cigarette until it had all but burnt away. I was just crushing it out beneath the platform heel of my boot when some car headlights appeared in the distance. They dipped down as the vehicle drove over a bump in the road and then lifted back up again.

'Someone's coming.'

'Yeah,' Andrea grinned knowingly. 'It's Phil, Sean and Taz.'

I knew the boys from the takeaway shop because they all worked there.

'I wonder what they want,' I replied.

Moments later, a grey car had pulled up alongside us and I watched as Taz pressed his finger against a button and the passenger's side window slowly slid down.

'Hello, you two. Fancy seeing you here,' he said, grinning.

Andrea's eyes darted from Taz's to the others and she smiled back.

'Yeah, what a surprise!' Phil said, smirking as he butted in from the driver's seat.

There was another man – a Pakistani man I'd never seen before – sitting in the back with Sean. I presumed he must be another friend of theirs. I was just wondering what to say when the back door swung open and Phil asked me to get in. In spite of his Westernised name, Phil was Pakistani, tall and had a goatee beard. Sean was the only white guy there but he was small, stocky and had a much bigger build than the others.

'Come on, Em, you look freezing, standing there in your jeans and little jumper. It's nice and warm in here. Look,' Phil said, twisting a dial on the dashboard, 'I'll put the heating up just for you.'

I looked over at Andrea, who nodded towards the car. I took it as a sign for us both to get in. Taz climbed out, as though he was making more room for us both inside. Just then, another car pulled up alongside. Its lights were snuffed and the engine cut out before an older Pakistani man appeared. The man was in his fifties and was wearing jeans and a jumper. I glanced into his car and I spotted a white apron on the back seat; I wondered if he was a chef.

'Hey,' Taz smiled, greeting the stranger as though he was an old friend.

He considered him warmly before the two shook hands.

By now, the prom was bitterly cold and I was desperate to escape the unrelenting sea breeze. The wind splintered against me like shards of ice; the cold sliced my skin and I rubbed my hands up and down my arms to try and get my blood flowing again.

'Come on,' Phil said, beckoning me inside the warm, cosy car.

The Pakistani man sitting in the back moved over to the other side as Sean got out so that I could sit in the middle.

'Come on, you're the smallest,' he joked.

The others laughed, and I felt like the schoolgirl I truly was as I climbed inside and waited for Andrea to join me. I waited a few seconds, but I realised she was still busy talking to Taz and the older man. I twisted my head to try and see where my friend was. As I did, I felt a hand grab my leg roughly. I automatically pushed it off and twisted again in my seat, trying to look for her. I felt another hand, and another. I pushed them all away. My eyes searched the darkness outside, looking for Andrea. I spotted three figures – Andrea's small, pale-yellow jacket, illuminated by the lights of the promenade, and two shadowy figures as the three of them walked away and disappeared behind the back of the ice-cream hut. I felt fingers, lots of fingers, pulling at my clothes. I turned in my seat but Sean had pulled the car door closed, which caused the interior light to go out. The car felt as dark as a cave, and I realised I was trapped. More hands and more fingers were on me, pulling at my top, grabbing the waistband of my trousers and snaking beneath my clothes.

'Get off me!' I screamed, as I tried to slap them all away.

I was busy wrestling all the hands away when Phil released the handbrake. Soon we were moving, away from Andrea, and along the prom. The car picked up speed as the outside whizzed past in a black and neon blur. The white-painted railings became one long, solid line as the car raced along the seafront road.

'I want to get out!' I cried. Fear rose at the back of my throat as though it might choke me. 'Please stop the car. I need to get out. I need to go back to Andrea!'

But Andrea was long gone; far behind us, along with Taz, the older man and the ice-cream kiosk. More hands started to grab me; one lifted my top, exposing my bra. Another managed to push its way between my legs.

'Please stop; please!' I screamed; hot tears streaming down my face.

But the men wouldn't listen because the men didn't care; I was just a piece of meat to them.

My breathing grew laboured and I felt so terrified that I thought I might pass out as the interior of the car and the men's faces and hands loomed in and out of view.

Suddenly, the car pulled to a halt and I was thrown sharply forward. I put out my hands to try and grip the headrest in front of me. But, without my hands to protect me, other hands – their hands – pulled and ripped at my clothing, trying to explore. I twisted and tried to break free, but all three men were pawing at me, pinning me down.

'Stop! Please stop!' I begged.

Tears flowed down the side of my temples, soaking my hairline, as they pinned me down on my back. I felt a greedy hand on my breast and another as it snaked its way down into my pants.

'No!' I tried to protest, but no one was listening.

I felt a tug on the waistband of my jeans so I grabbed it to try and hoist them back up. But one of the men pinned my wrists against the back seat. Then I felt other hands as they tried to pull my trousers and my knickers down. I tasted the acid bile of vomit at the back of my throat as my breathing became shallower. Panic engulfed me. Hot breath brushed against my skin as someone – their dead body weight – crushed me.

'Please don't, please don't!' I begged again and again, but all I heard was laughter.

'Go on, son!' the other men called out and jeered as Phil pinned me down.

I lifted both arms and tried to push him off, but I wasn't strong enough.

I was crying my eyes out but no one could hear; my pleas had been drowned out by the cheers and calls of the men.

They began to paw at my body and pull at my clothes like a pack of wild animals.

'Please! Please, take me back to my friend. Please!'

'Get off her; it's my turn!' a voice called angrily. I couldn't be sure who it belonged to because I'd clamped my eyes shut to try and block out what was happening. Fear had rendered me almost blind and my mind had short-circuited, blanked out and shut down. I felt the dead weight shift as someone pulled Phil off me. I gasped a grateful lungful of air – my ribs crushed and bruised.

'My turn!' a voice shouted.

'No! We agreed; it's mine.'

From nowhere, an argument broke out as the men began to fight amongst themselves.

I felt a surge of strength and willed myself to do something.

Run! You can try and escape this! I told myself as a survival instinct kicked in.

Drawing my knees up against my body, I quietly lifted myself into a sitting position as the men continued to argue between the front and back seats. They were rowing over who would be the first to have sex with me.

Get out! Get out of the car and run!

I twisted slowly so that I was seated against the side of the back door. The car was dark but I could still make them out; Phil, Sean and the unknown man I now knew was called Mo. Phil and Sean were busy pushing each other aggressively.

'You said I could go first!'

'No; we agreed, it was my turn!'

My eyes darted to the silver inside door release handle. With the men still busy I gripped the waistband of my jeans in one hand and, with the other, tugged the handle until the door had swung open. Somehow I managed to lift myself from sitting to standing within seconds, and soon I was running; running as fast as I could.

Run! You've got to run!

I cursed my stupid platform-heeled boots for slowing me up. Those and quaking legs made it feel as though I was trying to wade through thick mud as I willed them to go faster.

Come on; come on! my brain screamed as my legs began to burn.

I felt adrenalin coursing through my veins, giving me an extra jolt to try and escape. I sprinted towards the ice-cream kiosk. I could just make it out in the far distance. If I could reach it, then I could reach Andrea. She was the only one who could help me now. It was fight or flight, and I knew I had to get away from these men before they really hurt me.

'Andrea!' I screamed.

Hot, terrified tears blinded me, but I kept running – to Andrea, to safety. I heard voices – men's voices – and the sound of car doors slamming behind me, but I didn't dare turn around. I spotted the empty swimming pool up ahead as it emerged from the shadows and loomed into view.

Just get to Andrea. Run! Run! Get to Andrea and everything will be allright, I said to myself, willing my body to keep going.

Even though the wind was icy my lungs burned with every breath I took; each one scorching my insides.

Run, run! my brain screamed.

'Emily, Em, come back …' I heard a voice shout into the night before being carried away by the breeze.

There was a crashing of waves against the shore – the white surf rolling in at the mouth of a roaring sea.

'Quick! Catch her. She's getting away!'

Multiple voices grew louder and louder as the men began to close in on me. I saw the sharp, hard edge of the swimming pool just up in front of me. I could almost smell its chlorine-soaked tiled walls …

Faster, faster! I panicked as my lungs began to struggle. My heart was pumping like a piston engine, willing my legs to work harder, faster.

If you can just make it to the swimming pool – the ice-cream kiosk isn't much further, I told myself.

I clenched my fists and pumped them back and forth, trying to gain new momentum as I ran against the black storm blowing inland from the sea. I could taste the salt air in my mouth. I gripped at my waistband as my trousers began to slip down.

I couldn't stop. I couldn't.

My legs felt cold and numb, as though they belonged to someone else.

'Come here, you little bitch!' It was Phil.

Don't turn around! Keep running. Keep going. Not much further ...

I pushed myself to try to run faster but it was impossible; my ankles kept buckling as the men closed in on me. A hand grabbed the back of my jumper, causing me to stumble and then fall to my knees.

'Why you running away?' Phil gasped, spitting out the words. His face was twisted with anger and I realised just how ugly he was. 'We're not finished with you yet.'

'Yeah,' Sean said, smirking as he began to unbuckle his belt. 'We all wanna have a go.'

I felt someone's hand hook beneath my armpit and pull me back up to my feet. But it was no good; my ankles collapsed as my body started to tremble.

'Walk, you stupid bitch!' It was Phil again.

I tried to walk, but I was so petrified and so overwhelmed with panic that I was struggling to even function. The car was parked way behind us and back along the promenade. My eyes darted around the darkness, wondering where they would rape me. I spotted some public toilets on my right and felt my mind go into a blind panic.

The toilets; they're going to rape me in the toilets!

My whole body was on full alert as the men pulled me past the toilets and, half-dragged, half-carried me over towards the empty toddlers' swimming pool. During the summertime the same pool would be full of children, splashing, playing and paddling in the cool, fresh, blue water. Some would wear water wings; others would jump in with inflatable floats watched over by concerned parents, but not now. Now it was nothing but an empty shell – the whole area deserted. Winter had arrived with an icy blast and the long heady days of summer with its sand, sea and ice cream had long gone. There was no smell of candyfloss and suntan cream, only the stench of putrid puddles and collected rainwater.

'Down in there,' one of the men said as I was unceremoniously dragged and thrown against the hard, pool floor. With my face pressed up against blue concrete, multiple hands worked together to anchor me down and pull off my jeans. I felt the safety of denim leave my skin as the cold bit against it. Somehow, I still had my knickers, although they'd been ripped at the sides and were clinging to my body by a thread. But it didn't matter; the men didn't care. Two of them pinned me down and proceeded to rape me at the same time.

'Yeah, you little bitch! You like that, don't you?' I heard one shout as the others jeered.

I turned my face to the side and tried not to breathe in the rot and decay of the empty swimming pool. Instead, I allowed myself to drift off and focus on anything but this. My mind felt like a helium balloon tethered to a string, held in the hand of a laughing child. I pictured other children, splashing around in the water, and imagined myself looking up at the sun high in a cheery cloudless, blue sky. If I concentrated hard enough, I could almost feel the sun scorching my skin; the sensation of weightlessness as my legs bobbed upwards and I floated in the water. In my mind's eye I could picture smiles and laughter of families gathered in the sunshine; the love and the happiness – the warm glow of glorious summer days. I tried everything I could to block it out. The men, their voices, the horrible grunts and groans they made as they held me there and raped me face down in the empty swimming pool. But even the sound of the waves crashing against the shore had been drowned out by them and my screams.

'ANDREA! ANDREA!' I called out to her, but I knew it was no good – my friend wasn't coming; I was all alone. There was no sunshine, children or laughter. There was no warm sun against my skin; there was nothing but white, hot pain searing through my body – its jagged edges slowly ripping me to pieces. I've never felt pain like it before or since. The side of my face and thighs and knees had been skinned – rubbed raw against the rough concrete. Phil and Sean had raped me together. Once they'd finished, I staggered to my feet and ran back to the car. But if I thought my ordeal was over then I was wrong. I was still sore and bleeding when I was raped again, only this time by Mo.

'Go on, my son!' one of the men shouted as they both cajoled him.

That night, I'd been held down, raped and ripped apart not by men, but by animals. I was just fourteen years old. They'd ignored my screams. I'd called for help, but no one had come to my aid. That night, my childhood and my virginity had been taken – stolen from me – in the most brutal and barbaric way imaginable.

CHAPTER FIVE

BINS AND BLOODIED
KNICKERS

My hands and body were still shaking, and hot, humiliated tears flooded my face as I pulled my clothes back on.

'Yeah!' Phil crowed, punching the air as though congratulating himself on a job well done.

I began to weep in the back seat of the car; I couldn't help it. I was shocked; battered, bloodied and bruised.

The other men stayed quiet, but Phil couldn't help himself.

'Just get your clothes on and shut up crying, you whitey slag!'

I lifted my head up and caught Sean's eye. He was white too but if I thought he might stick up for me then I was mistaken. It was a pack mentality – kill or be killed. Sean turned to look out of the window as I felt another piece of me die inside.

'Look,' Phil said, laughing and pointing at my chest. 'Who did that, bro?'

I glanced down and noticed a big red bite mark at the top of my chest; someone had bitten me so hard that it was bleeding. I'd felt so sore between my legs that I hadn't even noticed it until now.

'Fucking whitey slag bag,' Phil said in disgust as he turned the ignition key.

The car fired into life as the engine roared and he flicked the headlights back on. The other two began to laugh, as though it had been one sick joke; it had, but the joke had been on me.

How could you have been so stupid? I cursed.

But none of that mattered now because all I wanted to do was lay down and die. I was sore, bleeding, and I felt utterly worthless.

'Come on,' Sean said, finally turning to face me. 'Cheer up, it might never happen.'

But it just had. They'd raped me. Each and every one of them had pinned me down and raped me. They knew what they'd done and so did I. A growing bitterness gnawed away inside.

'Take me back to Andrea. I want to go back to my friend.'

'No problem,' Phil replied, lighting up a spliff, puffing out the smoke from his cheeks. He took a long drag and handed it over to Sean. 'Whatever the whitey slag wants.'

The car spun around and soon we were heading back to where we'd started from. A knot of anxiety balled inside the pit of my stomach as we passed the swimming pool. I couldn't even look at it; I couldn't witness the place where it had happened. Instead, I clamped my eyes shut until I was certain we had driven past. The car screeched to a sudden halt and I was thrown forward in the back seat. An excruciating pain shot up from between my legs. The pain was sharp, as though someone had poured vinegar into my internal wounds – everything stinging and aching. There was a duller pain in my hips and my whole pelvis felt heavy, as though something was dragging it down.

'Here we are,' Phil announced.

Sean opened my door from his front seat, and a hand – I presumed Mo's – pushed me out, like a piece of rubbish, as I stumbled out onto the promenade.

'Hiya,' Andrea said, her eyes glinting underneath the ornate iron prom lights. They darted between me and the men as though she was trying to second guess what had happened.

'What took you so long?' Taz complained, before climbing into my seat.

There was a blast of the horn – a kind of celebratory toot – as the car and my three rapists pulled away and sped off into the night. I was numb with shock, but I stood there and watched as the back lights became two small, red dots in the distance. The car indicated, turned, and disappeared out of sight.

'Bye then,' the middle-aged Pakistani man said to Andrea.

His voice startled me because I'd forgotten all about him. He waved a cheery goodbye, got back inside his car, and drove off.

Andrea smiled weakly and then strolled over towards me. Linking her arm through mine, she turned to look at me because I couldn't stop shaking; I was still in shock.

'Christ, Em, you're freezing!' she chirped, rubbing a concerned hand up and down my arm to try and warm me up. I pulled away; I didn't want to be touched by anyone, not even a friend.

'Don't!'

I looked down at myself for the very first time; my white Playboy bunny sweatshirt had been ripped and my jeans were splattered with God only knows what. I caught Andrea looking too; it was obvious what had just happened.

'Where were you? Why did you leave me?' I croaked, trying to stem my tears.

My voice was barely a whisper, but I wasn't angry with her – I was still dazed and confused by what had just happened. I just couldn't make sense of it.

Andrea seemed awkward, even a little embarrassed, as she tried to search for the right words.

'I heard you scream but I couldn't get to you, Em. I swear!'

Her body language changed from normal to apologetic.

'I didn't know what to do, I swear! I didn't know how to help you, Em. You've got to believe me!'

I wanted to. I wanted to believe that my friend – the only real friend I had in the world – wouldn't have left me to my own fate.

'Here, are you sore?' she asked gently. 'Did they hurt you?'

Her concern made me let go of my resolve and break down.

'I think I'm bleeding,' I whispered, my eyes brimming with tears. 'You know, I'm bleeding down there. Everything hurts, Andrea – everything.'

My friend wrapped a concerned arm around my shoulders as I dissolved into a sobbing heap.

'Listen, do you think you can make it back to my house?'

I thought of Mum and Dad, curled up at home in front of the TV with my little sister. I desperately wanted to go home and get washed but I'd already told Mum I'd be staying at Andrea's. Besides, I couldn't go home with my clothes all ripped and bloody.

'Yes, I think so. But what will I do? What can I wear for college tomorrow?'

Andrea's mood brightened at this. She straightened up and began to take control of the situation.

'My clothes; you can borrow something from me.'

Then I remembered.

'No, wait. I've got a few spares in my locker, but I can't wear this,' I said, tugging at my ripped sweatshirt.

Somehow, although there was no weight on her, Andrea managed to prop me up against her and, with her arm supporting me, we stumbled back towards her house. Every step I took felt like agony as the pain continued to sear through me; each step a reminder of what had just happened.

'That's it, Em, not much further,' she encouraged.

But the half-mile walk had felt like a marathon, and I winced with every step. As we reached her back door, Andrea turned to me.

'Shush! You need to be quiet. I don't want my mum and dad to see you like this.' She gestured her hand up and down me. 'We'll have to sneak in the back and upstairs to my bedroom, okay?'

I nodded because I knew I didn't have much choice. I tried to picture myself as Andrea did, standing in torn and muddy clothes. I realised that I must have looked a bit of a state.

'Can I have a shower or a bath?' I asked, wiping my arm against my face to try and brush away the last of my tears.

Andrea shook her head.

'No, my parents are a bit funny about things like that,' she said coldly.

I felt like crying all over again; I was so desperate to scrub them off – the men who had left their scent on me – that I felt like clawing away my own skin. But instead, we made our way to her bedroom where she lent me one of her thick jumpers. My body was still shaking so much that I had to hold my hands in my lap just to try and keep them still. A little later, Andrea began to broach what had happened at the prom and asked what the men had done to me.

'Did you have sex then?' she asked bluntly.

I couldn't look at her. My anger had morphed into some kind of guilt; my fear replaced by humiliation and shame. Instead, I remained quiet.

Andrea nodded, lit a fag and pushed open her bedroom window. She blew a long, grey plume of smoke out into the inky black night – the wind immediately dispersed it.

'Thought so,' she said.

I looked up at her.

'Why?'

'Because Phil once raped me.'

Her words hung between us, but right now it was Andrea who couldn't look at me. She turned away and stared blankly out at the night as though she was back in that moment – the night Phil had done the exact same thing to her.

'When?'

I sat up straight on her bed, demanding to know. A rage built up inside me; the bastard had done this before!

But Andrea was still lost in thought.

'What?' she asked, turning briefly before looking back out at the night. 'Oh, ages ago.'

A gasp escaped my mouth and I shook my head in disbelief. I thought back to Andrea and how she hadn't climbed inside the car.

Had she known what Phil and his mates might do to me?

I shook the idea from my head almost as soon as I'd thought of it.

No, of course she hadn't. Andrea was my friend – she'd never do that to me.

I felt guilty for even thinking such a horrible thing. Instead, I looked over at a crumpled plastic bag I'd thrown next to her bin in the corner of the bedroom. Inside were my ripped top, muddy jeans and blood-splattered knickers. I felt my throat constrict with panic.

'What the hell am I going to do with them? I can't take them home; Mum would kill me!'

Andrea thought for a moment, crushed out her fag and threw it out of the window.

'We'll put them in a bin, on the way to college in the morning. That's what I usually do.'

'You do?'

'Yeah. Course I do.'

Later that evening, I was still so shaken that I couldn't stop crying, so Andrea decided to call Childline.

'They'll know what to do,' she insisted, trying to reassure me.

But before she'd had the chance to speak, she lost her nerve and put down the phone. I was emotionally shattered and still trying to make sense of what had happened. I replayed what the three men had done to me back at the prom. That evening I fell into a fitful night's sleep and relived my ordeal bit by bit. If I'd cried out during the night then Andrea never mentioned it. Instead, we slept top to tail in her single bed. My jeans had been stinking, so I'd bundled them in the plastic bag along with my underwear and borrowed a pair of leggings and knickers from her. Both were absolutely tiny and dug in against my skin. The following morning I woke early and lay there, staring at the children's wallpaper covering the wall. It had felt so far removed from the night before that I wondered if I'd even imagined it. But the dull ache from between my legs told me otherwise. I glanced down at my ripped T-shirt; blood from the bite mark on my chest, just above my breast, had seeped through into the white collar, staining it red.

Andrea was still fast asleep as I lay there staring at the blood and the wallpaper. I wondered if that's what sex was supposed to be like. The pain between my legs was excruciating but I desperately needed a wee. I steeled myself and nipped to the toilet but when I tried to pee nothing happened. I panicked that I'd been damaged for life. I was only fourteen and, although I knew how to run drugs over county lines, I didn't have a clue about sex.

Eventually Andrea woke, but I wanted to get my own clothes from my locker, so even though it was still early we headed over for college. On our way there I grabbed the bag containing my muddied clothes and blood-stained knickers, and threw it into a street bin. Getting rid of the evidence made me feel better. It was as though they now belonged to the past – out of sight and out of mind. Thankfully, Andrea didn't ask me any more questions about that night. If anything, she played it down.

'Well, if you were a virgin, you're not any more!' she said, laughing, as though the whole thing had been funny.

My stomach cramped inside and I felt like I wanted to die. Andrea noticed.

'Look, it's just sex, Em. That's what men are like. We've all been there. The first time is always the worst but it gets easier, I promise.'

She went on to explain how sex often hurts, especially at first, but I'd soon get used to it.

'Like I have.'

But it hadn't felt like sex – it had been rape. The men had raped me. However, Andrea was my best friend and right then she meant more to me than anyone else in the world. I trusted her; I was naive, but she was older than me so I decided she must be right – this must be what happened when you first start having sex. Although in the back of my mind a nagging voice told me it had been wrong – those men had held me down and had sex with me against my will. I tried to block it out to try and fool myself that I hadn't been a victim.

No, I told myself. I'd finally had sex, lost my virginity, and now I was a grown woman, making grown-up decisions. Sadly, the reality was that I was absolutely nothing of the sort. I was just a terrified child, utterly desperate for someone to notice and rescue me from what had now become my life.

'Listen, we need to get you the morning after pill, Em,' Andrea insisted, interrupting my thoughts.

'What's that?'

She shook her head as though I still had so much to learn.

'You take it to stop yourself from getting pregnant. I presume they didn't use anything, did they?'

I looked at her blankly.

'You know, rubbers, condoms?'

I shook my head.

They didn't stop to even consider that, I thought bitterly.

'Well, that's it then; you definitely need the MAP,' she decided.

Andrea led me towards the hospital in the middle of town, where a nurse told us we needed to go to a health centre situated around the side of the building. Andrea opened up the door and pushed me inside.

'Whatever you do, don't give them your real name!' she hissed as she turned and waited outside.

I started to walk down a short corridor, towards the receptionist, feeling utterly terrified. However, the thought of being pregnant scared me more and propelled me towards the reception. Standing behind the counter was a stern-looking woman, wearing a dark navy cardigan. She had blonde hair that she'd dragged back into a harsh ponytail.

'Yes, can I help you?' she asked, looking directly at me.

I wanted the earth to swallow me whole; I felt so out of place and sick with nerves. I thought how strange my fear was. I'd run drugs for Barry since the age of eleven. I'd been inside some horrible dives over the years, some that had been no better than doss houses, but I'd never been anywhere like this before.

'I … I …'

The receptionist looked me up and down impatiently, waiting for me to elaborate.

'Why are you here?' she finally snapped.

'For the MAP!'

The woman stared at me blankly.

'The morning after pill,' I said, correcting myself.

'Right, I see. And your name?'

I racked my brains trying to think of a name that wasn't my own.

'Ivy.'

The woman eyed me again; it was obvious she didn't believe a word.

'Ivy what?'

'Jones,' I said, thinking of the most Welsh surname I knew.

'I see, and where do you live … Miss Jones?'

I gave her a false address, hoping she wouldn't ask me to repeat it because my mind had gone completely blank.

'Right then, er, Ivy …'

I cringed inside; I looked nothing like an Ivy – I was far too young.

'If you'd like to take a seat over there, the nurse will call your name.'

I turned to see a row of seats with three other girls already waiting to go in. All of them looked older than me, and I felt ridiculously young as I took an empty seat next to them. One looked up but I shot her such a filthy look that she stared back down at the magazine in her lap.

Before long, a nurse had called me into a tiny room. It backed onto the side of the building and I spotted Andrea, still waiting, through the window. At one point the nurse got up and left to fetch a pregnancy test kit, so I stood up, tapped on the window and signalled for Andrea to come inside.

Suddenly the door opened and the nurse caught me still standing at the window.

'Sorry,' I said, grinning sheepishly. 'It's my friend. She was waiting for me outside; she's just coming in.'

She nodded as though she'd seen it all before.

'Right, Ivy. I need you to take this and pee onto the stick part of it for me. Do you understand?'

'Yes.'

'Good, now, the toilets are just outside this room on the right. When you're done, I'd like you to come back in here.'

'OK.'

By the time I left the room Andrea was already waiting outside the door.

'I need to do this. Come to the loo with me,' I said, showing her the pregnancy test kit.

'Oh, they always make you do one of these before they'll give you the MAP,' she said knowingly.

Andrea was so comfortable being there that she followed me back inside the room. I expected the nurse to say something or tell Andrea to wait outside, but she didn't seem to care.

'Well, your test is negative so I can give you the morning after pill.'

I looked over at my friend and beamed.

'However,' the nurse said, stony-faced, 'I'd like you to use protection in future, Ivy. Do you understand?'

Andrea let out a snort of laughter. It took me a minute to figure out why, and then I realised she was laughing at my made-up name.

'Yes.'

The nurse explained how the morning after pill worked and gave me a tablet to swallow. Then she handed Andrea and me a huge bag of condoms as she completed her paperwork. But, with my false name and address, I knew none of it would be traceable back to me. I expected the nurse to ask me how many men I'd had sex with, but she never did. Instead, she seemed annoyed; as though she had better things to do than give a fourteen-year-old girl the morning after pill.

As we left the room, Andrea's long, mousy hair fell forward as she grabbed a handful of leaflets on the side and we ran giggling out of the sexual health centre.

'What are you going to do with all those?' I asked as I spotted the stash of leaflets in her hand.

'This!' she said, throwing them up into the air. They billowed up and outwards, before fluttering gently back down to the ground.

'Andrea!' I screeched.

We pissed ourselves laughing and ran off across town and back towards college. The doors were locked so we knocked until the caretaker answered. He was a nice guy, so we managed to persuade him to let us in.

'You two are early this morning,' he said, smiling, as he unlocked the door.

Once inside, we went straight to the toilet where I bought sanitary towels from the dispenser.

'How do you feel?' Andrea asked, applying some lip gloss in the mirror.

'Sore. I think I'm coming on my period. I've got cramps.'

Andrea flicked a hand through her mousey hair.

'Yeah, that'll be the MAP. It does that.'

Although I'd been held down and attacked multiple times, after speaking with Andrea I convinced myself it must have been my fault.

You need to be more careful next time.

I realised that if I continued to hang around with her then there would be a next time. I knew it for sure because of the company she kept. Looking back, I should have walked away then, but I was just so desperate to be liked. Andrea valued me as a friend, and I found that totally addictive. I'd never had a best friend before and now that she'd helped me through the most difficult morning of my life I felt we'd bonded. We were tied together because now we shared a secret, and we promised to keep that secret as we made our way to the classroom and our first lesson.

The morning after pill seemed to bring on my period; it felt much heavier than normal. The ensuing cramps and pain were hard to deal with and, in the days that followed, I found it almost impossible to concentrate. I was reminded of what had happened every time I sat down. I wanted to cry but I told myself I mustn't. I had to be strong – I had to be grown-up. Of course, I didn't say a word to Mum even though I'm certain she must have noticed because I was much quieter than usual. Afterwards, my emotions felt all jumbled up inside. I'd wanted to grow up, just not this quickly. It had been my first sexual encounter and I wasn't sure if it had actually been rape. I had no one other than Andrea to talk to and she had such a skewed view on sex that she made it sound normal. I didn't fully understand the enormity of what had just happened to me. I also felt trapped because I knew if I made a fuss and didn't go along with it then I'd lose my best friend, and she was far too precious to lose. Before the night at the prom, I'd been having so much fun that I never wanted it to end. Even though I was still a child, I wanted to share vodka, smoke fags, and enjoy spliffs with the older girls because they seemed so much cooler. They were all having sex, even Michelle, and she was the same age as me. I thought it must be normal – a girl my age to be having sex – even though it was anything but. After the prom, I felt my confidence begin to slip, but I was determined not to let it beat me. It couldn't, because now I had Andrea. I looked up to my best friend because she was the only person who knew what it felt like to be me. She'd found a way to 'fit in' and so could I. I wanted to be mature and sophisticated like her, and for everyone to like me. I wanted to have lots of friends but, most of all, I wanted to impress Andrea so that I didn't lose her friendship. Ashley was still my friend but she'd moved on. These college girls were all I had.

CHAPTER SIX

BARRY

I thought I'd seen the last of Barry after Angela had kicked him out, but I was wrong. One afternoon Carys asked me if I wanted to go back to her house after college. As we approached her street, I experienced a bit of déjà vu.

'Hang on, I've been here before,' I remarked as we walked along the familiar street and turned the corner into her own.

'Oh my God, Carys! I know someone who lives down here. He lives right here, in this street. That's his house there – the one with the yellow fence.'

Carys looked at me a little gobsmacked.

'Bryn?'

I nodded as I pictured big, fat Bryn squashed onto his small, brown sofa.

'Yes, that's him. Why, do you know him?'

'Know him?' Carys said, beginning to laugh. 'He's my next-door neighbour!'

One hand shot straight to my mouth. I tugged at her sleeve.

'I used to know someone who sold him drugs.'

'Yeah, that's where I get all mine – from Bryn. Come on, let's go and say hello.'

Apprehensively, I followed her inside. I wasn't sure I wanted to revisit my old life.

Bryn's house hadn't changed at all; it was still a cramped, dark and seedy shit hole – just as I'd remembered it.

'Hey, Bryn.'

'Hey, Carys.'

'Bryn,' Carys said, moving to one side, 'I've brought someone here to see you.'

He glanced up as I stepped out of the shadow of the doorway.

'Fucking hell! It's Em, isn't it?'

I smiled and nodded.

'All right, Bryn,' I said following my friend, who had walked over to the sofa and plonked herself down.

Bryn shook his head as though he couldn't quite believe it.

'Last time I saw you, Em, you were this high,' he said, holding his hand a few feet off the ground. 'And you was with Barry.'

'Yeah, well, I've not seen Barry for years, have I?' I said, taking a packet of fags out of my pocket.

Bryn reeled back in surprise.

'Really? Well he lives round here now, you know.'

I sat up bolt straight in my chair.

'Here?'

'Yeah, he's just over the back from me. Lives with a

woman called Pauline. Here, you should go over and say hello.'

But I didn't want to. In truth, I was glad to finally have Barry out of my life. Instead, Carys and I bought a bag of pills and some weed off Bryn, which we smoked together in his front room. After a while, we got up to leave.

'I'll tell Barry I've seen you,' Bryn insisted, his fat neck wobbling as he spoke.

'Yeah,' I replied, smiling weakly.

As far as I was concerned, that part of my life had been and gone, and I didn't work for anyone – not any more.

Not long afterwards, once we'd run out of weed and pills, we called around Bryn's house again. There were a few different blokes inside; one had brought a tattoo machine and Bryn was desperate to test it out.

'Come on, girls. At least one of you let me try it out. Go on, it'll be a laugh!'

But there was no way I was letting fat Bryn near my skin. Eventually, Carys agreed it would be a bit of a laugh, so Bryn and two of his mates took turns to give her a tattoo on her back as a present for her fifteenth birthday. The tattoo was crude and amateurish; it was so bad that I didn't have a clue what it was meant to be.

'It looks good,' Bryn lied, as he dug the needle in a bit deeper.

I wasn't sure what to say; *should I do something to make him stop?* But what would be worse – a badly drawn tattoo the length of your back, or a half-finished one? I was just about to open my mouth when the back door swung open and in walked Barry.

'All right, Em!' he said, greeting me as though we were long-lost friends.

'All right, Barry,' I responded with a smile, although it wasn't sincere and it didn't reach my eyes.

'Has Bryn told you I live over the back there?' He gestured with his thumb towards the back of his house through the kitchen window.

I nodded.

'Yeah, I've been meaning to come round.'

Now it was my turn to lie.

'Well, you know where I am if you need anything?'

Barry didn't need to elaborate; I knew exactly what he meant – drugs. I think he'd realised that Bryn had been muscling in on potential new clients. Bryn looked up and then back down at the half-done tattoo, trying to concentrate. The needle continued to buzz as Carys's screams reached fever pitch.

A week or so later, we nipped around to see Barry at his house. Now he knew we were in the market for drugs I was wary of buying them directly from Bryn. I'd witnessed what Barry had done with Bryn's axe, so I knew what he was capable of.

We watched as he weighed out, cut and handed me a block of weed and a bag of pills.

'Thanks, Barry. How much do I owe?' I asked, digging a hand into the inside of my jacket pocket.

'What? Oh, no charge.'

I was flummoxed.

'What? But I must owe you something?'

Barry rested back in his chair. Bryn had already told us that Barry shared the house with his girlfriend; but she was out at work which meant Carys and I were all alone with him. Barry considered me for a moment as though trying to weigh up the situation and then he spoke.

'Okay, I'll tell you what; instead of you paying me for that, how about a blow job off the pair of you? Not just one, both?' he leered, licking his lips.

I was mortified and looked over towards Carys in horror.

'I'll do it,' she agreed, which kind of left me with no option.

Deep down, I knew it was wrong, but once she'd started it had been expected of me. I felt sick throughout, but once we'd finished we took our pills and weed and left. Sadly, once he'd made us do it he knew he would be able to ask again and again.

Afterwards, Carys's behaviour seemed to change. I loved her; she was so much fun to be with, but she and Andrea had never seen eye to eye. Andrea would slag her off behind her back, even though she'd done nothing wrong. I felt as though Andrea was trying to put my loyalty to the test. Carys was always smuggling alcohol into college – we all were, given half the chance – and we would share it between us. However, one day she brought in a bottle of vodka. She'd drunk most of it before the first lesson, so when one of the lecturers had a go at her she gave as good as she'd got back. Not long afterwards, Carys was kicked off the course for her behaviour.

During the lesson we would learn how to work alongside children. There was a nursery attached to the college and we would read, play and look after small children. I'd never been maternal, but I didn't mind looking after other people's kids as long as I could give them back.

I was fifteen when I met Jac. He was training to become a mechanic. Soon, Jac and I started going out together. At nineteen, he was four years older than me, but I didn't care because he was into booze and drugs so we had lots in common. The first time I had sex with Jac I was so off my face on some pills that I could only recall bits of it. I was worried sex might trigger flashbacks to the prom, which was why I'd taken the drugs in the first place – to give me courage and mask my fear. Jac was great but he had this crazy mate called Huw who had a box of knives that he'd collected and treasured with his life. Huw was completely bonkers but the drugs made him even worse and we were never sure what he'd do next. One night, Carys and I were sitting smoking a spliff with Jac and Huw when he suddenly brought out his box of knives to show us. He kept them inside their own special silver metal box on wheels.

'Look at these, then. What do you think to this one?' Huw said. The edge of the metal glinted against the light.

He looked so serious that Carys and I began to snigger over in the corner.

Jac shot me a look that told me to be quiet, but I couldn't help myself.

'What's funny?' Huw snapped, looking over at us giggling on the sofa.

'Nothing ...' Carys replied, before bursting out laughing.

It was the trigger Huw needed. Before we had the chance to move, he was on top of us both, holding the biggest knife against Carys's neck. Nobody moved and the happy atmosphere melted into a stifling claustrophobic tension.

'Listen, we weren't laughing at you,' I said, trying to reason with him.

I felt the cold edge of the sharp blade graze the soft skin of my neck as he switched it from Carys to me.

'Stop it, Huw. It isn't funny.'

It was Jac. Huw looked over towards him a little startled. But he was soon back on the defensive.

'Well, these little slags think it's funny, don't you?'

Carys and I shook our heads. We didn't think it was funny. In fact, the situation was the furthest from funny that you could get.

'No, we don't ... sorry, Huw ...' Carys stammered.

I looked in Huw's eyes as he held the blade defiantly against my neck.

'And what about you, Em? You think I'm funny? You think this – these knives – are funny?'

I wanted to shake my head but the blade was so close up against my throat that I could feel metal biting into my skin.

'No,' I whispered, 'I don't think they're funny.'

Huw pulled the knife away and went to sit back down. I thought I was going to pass out. It was obvious he was absolutely nuts; it was also clear that he had no sense of humour whatsoever. Afterwards, no one mentioned Huw's knives ever again.

I would travel to college with Jac on the bus every morning. But then he passed his driving test and so he'd drive us in. I don't know why, but it didn't even enter my head to use contraception. Jac was my first proper boyfriend, so it seemed natural to just go along with things. It wasn't until I was in my second year at college that I started to feel a bit sick. One morning, my sister Lucy found me hanging my head over the toilet bowl.

'What's wrong, Em?'

I got to my feet and looked at my reflection in the mirror of the bathroom cabinet. My face was washed out, as though all the blood had been drained from me.

'I dunno. I just feel a bit weird. I've not had my period for four months, but don't tell Mum, will you?'

Lucy shook her head; I knew that, at twelve, she was too young to understand what it meant anyway.

'I won't, promise.'

But I was still feeling peculiar as I walked into my first lesson of the day. That morning we had a particularly hard-faced tutor called Yvonne. She noticed me squirming in my seat throughout the lesson and came over to ask what was wrong.

'My period's late, Yvonne,' I confided, hoping that she might be able to put my mind at rest or offer me some helpful advice. She did neither. Instead, she looked me up and down as though I was the shit on her shoe.

I felt like crying. So, when one of the girls in my class offered me a can of Red Bull, I took it, threw my head back and glugged it down.

'Em, it's got Bacardi in it.'

But I didn't give a shit. Instead, I wiped my mouth with my sleeve and asked for more.

During the first break a group of us wandered up to the nearby football club, but as I got to my feet I felt a sharp pain bolt through my abdomen.

'Come on, Em,' Andrea said, trying to hurry me along. 'We don't have long.'

By now my stomach had begun to contract.

'You okay, Em?'

It was Bronwyn, another girl from my class.

'Yeah,' I grimaced, trying to disguise the pain, 'I'm fine.'

I slid my textbooks into my bag and followed the others out. However, by the time we returned I was so crippled with pain that I could barely think straight.

'I'm just nipping to the bog,' I told the group as I dashed into the disabled loo, situated between the boys' and girls' toilets.

Andrea, Bronwyn and two boys were all standing outside, drinking Red Bull and vodka. Others had mixed it with Bacardi, but they were guzzling it down fast before the next class.

There was a table right by the toilet door, and that's when it happened – a pain so crippling that I bent over double in agony.

'Oh God, help me; somebody help me!' I screamed.

A boy called Nigel, who had been standing outside, heard and came rushing in. He saw me crouching with a hand pressed against my stomach; he was unsure what to do, so he went to fetch Andrea.

'Oh fuck, Em! What's happened? Are you all right?' she gasped, standing in the doorway looking over at me.

But I wasn't; I was anything but.

'Quick, help me up. I'll be fine,' I grimaced, trying to put on a brave face. She hooked her arm underneath mine and pulled me up to my feet. I gasped and leant against the table for support. It took several deep breaths just to feel a little better.

'Are you okay?'

I nodded and gritted my teeth.

'Yes, I'll be fine,' I insisted.

But, moments later, a crippling agony ripped through my body.

'Oh fuck!' I gasped.

'What is it? What's wrong?'

'Oh God,' I began to sob as I staggered towards the loo.

And that's when it happened. I slumped down onto the toilet, clutching at my stomach, as though all the stuffing had been taken out of me. The pain was indescribable – as though I'd been kicked repeatedly in the guts by someone wearing rugby boots. Andrea was so freaked out that she ran to try and find Nigel to ask him to bring an older girl on our course to help. In the meantime I clamped my eyes shut and winced silently, trying desperately not to howl out loud. There was blood – lots of blood. I wiped myself and used a sanitary towel but as soon as I got to my feet more blood gushed from me. I looked down at my knickers – they were covered, and so were my jeans. I had bled through everything.

'Christ!' It was Andrea. She was back, but she couldn't stop staring at all the blood. 'Em, what the fuck is it? What's happened?'

My whole body was trembling as I looked up at her.

'My period; it's late,' I mumbled, as I saw the blood – so much blood. 'What am I going to do?' I said, starting to cry.

'Em, you must be having a miscarriage!'

I shook my head. She was wrong; she had to be. I was only fifteen.

'But the morning after pill; I always take it,' I explained, in between sobs.

'But not with Jac, have you?'

And that's when I realised – Andrea was right. I'd not taken precautions with Jac because he was my boyfriend.

'Oh Christ, Andrea, what am I going to do?' I said, breaking down completely.

There was panic in Andrea's eyes as she looked all around, trying to work out what to do for the best.

'Clean yourself up; do what you can. Nigel's bringing Stacey; she'll know what to do.'

Although we waited, Stacey didn't show. Instead, Andrea came with me as I half-walked, half-staggered along the corridor towards the room of our lecturer, Yvonne. Andrea checked that no one was coming as I shuffled over towards the door. With my bloodstained clothes I felt utterly ashamed and embarrassed, but there was no time for that now. I had to get help. I lifted a hand and knocked urgently against the door.

'Come in,' Yvonne called.

We opened the door but I didn't dare go into the room. Instead, I hung back, hovering behind Andrea.

'What now?' Yvonne huffed.

'Can I speak to you, please?'

'Are you going to join us in the lesson today, Emily, or what?' she asked sarcastically. She was sorting through some paperwork and didn't even bother to lift her eyes to look at me.

'It's not that,' I said, my voice sounding all flustered. 'I think I've just had a miscarriage back there,' I said, pointing behind me, 'in the disabled toilet.'

I stood to one side of Andrea so that Yvonne could see the blood patch that had seeped into my jeans, between my legs.

She looked downwards and then back up at me.

'Well, that's what you get for fucking about, isn't it?'

Everything went stonily quiet. Neither Andrea nor I knew what to say because her words had taken us both by surprise. My mouth fell open in shock. I hadn't expected much sympathy from Yvonne, but I'd expected compassion. I received neither. But she still hadn't finished with me. She put both hands on her desk and considered me as I hovered in the doorway.

'Anyway, nothing should be going up there. Things should be coming out, not going in!' she added nastily. 'That is all,' she said, waving me away and out of her room.

At that moment, Stacey arrived. She was gasping and out of breath because she'd been running all over college looking for us.

'Lend Emily your jacket,' Yvonne ordered. 'She's had, erm, a bit of an accident.'

I wanted the ground to open up as Stacey looked down in horror at the blood. She silently handed over her jacket so that I could tie it around my waist to cover the worst of it. I wasn't sure what I should do next, but it was obvious I couldn't sit in lessons like that.

'Go and see Wendy, and Stacey,' Yvonne said, pointing to the older girl, 'you go with her.'

Wendy was the course leader and her office was just along the bottom of the corridor.

'What happened?' Stacey asked as we walked along and stood outside Wendy's door.

I lifted a hand to knock against it.

'I think I've just had a miscarriage, but don't tell Wendy. I'll tell her I've just got a really bad period.'

I'd decided following Yvonne's reaction that I didn't want any more of the staff to know what had happened. Instead, I told Wendy I'd come on a really heavy period and was suffering from a crushing headache; she was as sympathetic as Yvonne had been.

'Very well, then I suggest you go outside and get some fresh air. There's a football game over on the sports field. You can go and watch that, and Stacey, you go with her,' she said, shooing us both out of her office.

Stacey wrapped her arm around me as we crossed over the field to watch the stupid game of football. I was shaking with both cold and shock, but I couldn't remove Stacey's jacket from my hips because then the whole college would have seen.

During the last break, Bronwyn came looking for us. She knew something was seriously wrong as soon as she saw me standing on the side of the pitch, crying.

'Christ, Em, what's up?' she asked, looking from me to Stacey.

'I think I've had a miscarriage, Bron.'

'Oh Christ, Em, come here,' she said, wrapping her arms around me.

I was so upset and shell-shocked that I'd totally forgotten the spare clothes I regularly stored in my locker. I always kept some just in case we decided to go out after college. It was Bron who reminded me.

'Fuck! I completely forgot.'

Thankfully, a friend had arranged to pick me up in his car later that night, so I went back to the loo and got changed before taking a swig from a bottle of vodka I also had stashed in there. Then I bundled my bloodied jeans back into the locker. The following day I threw them into an anonymous bin in the town centre, so that no one would ever trace them back to me.

Unsurprisingly, my relationship with Jac didn't last much longer. Although I thought he was my boyfriend, it turned out that he'd been having sex with Carys and some other girls around town. Not long afterwards I confronted Carys about it.

'I didn't know he was with you; I swear!'

I trusted Carys; I knew she wasn't lying because Jac had been kinky and was always asking me to have threesomes. I'd refused, so he'd roped in Carys and a mate of his. But he was kinky in other ways too – he liked people to see him perform. Sometimes his boss, who ran a pub, would come along to watch us have sex before rewarding me with crisps and Bacardi.

'He did the same with me,' she admitted.

She was mortified and I believed her more than I believed Jac, so, together, we called at his flat to confront him. But Jac was furious and he locked us inside his flat and refused to let us out. With nothing else to do, Carys and I got off our faces on phetamine – it was the first time I'd ever tried it; I loved the buzz so much that it started me off on another rocky road of addiction. We were so high that we decided to steal his car. Carys, who was still taking driving lessons, drove it down a massive hill and crashed it into a fence. My life was coming off the rails in more ways than one.

Afterwards, in a bid to numb all the pent-up anger and anxiety, my drug and alcohol use went off the scale. One day, Andrea and I met a group of boys and had sex with them all. Once again, as it had been down at the prom, the sex had been brutal. We were both left bloodied and bruised. Andrea was so upset that she pulled me into a nearby phone box and rang Childline to tell them what had just happened. I watched the colour drain from her face – her eyes darting over to mine.

'What do you mean it's not confidential?' she shouted down the phone. 'I thought everything I told you was confidential.'

But the person on the other end of the line explained that in some cases the service would break confidentiality if it felt a child was at risk.

'Right, I see,' Andrea replied curtly before slamming down the phone.

'Come on, leg it!'

So we did; all the way across the supermarket car park. We stood, waiting and watching from the shadows as two policemen arrived at the phone box minutes later.

'Fuck, that was a close shave!' Andrea gasped, still trying to catch her breath

After that, we didn't trust anyone. My mum had just got me a mobile phone, but now I knew never to try and ring from that. We knew we were stuck. If Childline couldn't help us without involving the police, then who could?

Without Carys at college, the only time I ever saw her was when I needed drugs.

One day we were sitting at Bryn's house smoking weed when this other man walked in with his girlfriend. They were selling coke and weed, and Bryn was keen to strike a deal. The man was called Ivor. His girlfriend, in particular, seemed really nice and offered to sell me and Carys drugs directly. I realised that she was the dealer and Ivor was her boyfriend and bodyguard. Ivor liked his weed and he smoked more than most, but he was also a show-off and a bit of a wanker. So I wasn't shocked when, a short while later, I heard he'd been busted. However, Ivor wasn't just a weed fiend; he was also a serving police officer, who worked as a detective in the CID!

Word had soon reached Bryn, who shook his head in disgust the next time I saw him.

'I couldn't believe it when I heard, Em. If they can bust Ivor, they can bust anyone,' Bryn said, lighting up a joint and taking a long drag to try and calm his nerves. 'Fucking disgusting, it is!'

I tried not to laugh. Ivor was known in the area for smoking dope and, as a copper, had regularly raided dealers down at the prom with a 'stop and search'. It was a well-known fact that he'd hand in the hard stuff at the station and keep the weed for himself.

'I don't know what the world's coming to; I really don't, nicking one of their own,' Bryn added.

There was, it seemed, a certain honour amongst thieves.

I'd begun to hang around with Andrea more. In many ways it helped tighten her control of me. A short while later she convinced me to go back to the takeaway shop where Phil, Sean and Taz worked and hung out.

'It's just sex, Em. They're our friends,' she reasoned.

I felt really scared the first time I saw them all again, but they acted so normal that I convinced myself I'd blown it all out of proportion. I was so desperate to have people in my life – I didn't care who – as long as I didn't have to be alone any more. Any attention – good or bad – was still attention.

A few days later, Andrea, Ruth and I went over to Mo's house. He didn't live very far from my friends, who thought he was a good guy. At one point Mo left the room to fetch something so I grabbed Andrea's arm and pulled her over towards me.

'Don't leave me with him, will you?'

'Of course I won't. Stop worrying.'

But we got drunk and smoked joints so, by the time other people had started to arrive, including Taz, their faces seemed to float in and out of the room.

'Come here,' Taz said at one point, dragging me over to sit on his lap.

The television, windows, everything began to bend in and out of shape as I felt my body being tugged down onto the sofa. But I felt safe because I could hear the other girls' voices in the room. However, it was a false sense of security; I drifted in and out of consciousness as Taz and then Mo proceeded to climb on top of me and rape me. When I came around, I was in a bedroom. I looked up at the clock on the wall; it was one o'clock and I had no idea how long I'd been there.

It had grown dark outside but a man who told me his name was Andy came into the bedroom. One minute he was talking to me, the next minute I fell unconscious through booze and drugs, so I'm not sure if he had sex with me.

Although Andrea had brought along a big bag of condoms, they remained unused. Afterwards, I convinced myself I was fine, that it had been a good night, and that this was what teenagers did. But a month or so later I discovered our names had been extensively passed between countless men, who had been told that we would have sex with them for free drugs. Soon, Carys began to meet men – not boys – to have sex with them, and I tagged along. The men – both Pakistani and white – would pay us for sex with drugs. We'd soon become addicted and our bodies craved drugs which we had to get in any way, shape or form, whatever the price. We'd started to sink below a level of depravity and there was no one there to catch us. I found myself on a tidal wave of abuse at the hands of men who should've known better. The unrelenting tide rose higher and higher until soon I couldn't stop it, even if I'd tried. By now I was sleeping with countless men, who gave me drugs, which would numb the pain of what they were doing to me. It had become a vicious cycle. I'd give Barry blow jobs for pills, and faceless white Welsh and Pakistani men sex for booze and drugs.

One day, Barry was going on a drug run and asked me if I'd go with him.

'Okay,' I agreed, even though I was worried; I'd not done a drug run with Barry for years but I knew he must have asked me for a reason.

Not long afterwards, his van drew up at our arranged pick-up point. With the radio blaring and us both smoking fags in the front, in many ways it had felt familiar, just like old times.

'Here we are,' Barry said, pulling up outside a massive converted barn in the middle of the Welsh countryside.

My mouth gaped open – it was the biggest house I'd ever seen.

'Come on,' he chirped.

He climbed out and went to knock on the door. A man answered and we followed him. Three other guys were inside. They seemed to be waiting for Barry, who pulled out a huge bag of cocaine. One man used a credit card to nudge it into two long, thin white lines on top of the polished mahogany table. Then all three began to snort it. Barry and I were just standing there and I wasn't sure what to do, so I asked if I could use the toilet.

'Sure, that door behind you, turn to the right, and it's straight across from you.'

'Thanks,' I smiled, rising from my chair.

In reality, I just wanted a good nosey round. The house was huge and had been finished to a high spec, with polished wooden floors and stripped wooden doors. I soon found the toilet and closed the door behind me, but it wouldn't lock. The latch was broken and, no matter how hard I tried, it just wouldn't click into place. Unsure what to do, I wedged the sole of my foot against it to keep it shut. But with Barry in the other room I felt safe. Afterwards I found my way back to the living room, where the men were still sampling Barry's finest cocaine. As soon as I entered, the room fell into a hush as though I'd interrupted something. An unsettling feeling nestled in the pit of my stomach, but I told myself I'd be fine; Barry had my back. But then he said he had to nip somewhere else.

'Don't worry, Em, I'll be back for you soon.'

The unsettled feeling twisted itself into a knot of anxiety as I watched him leave. Barry never left me. Never.

'But I could come with you …' I said, trying to run after him as he walked towards the door.

The men's eyes darted between themselves as though everyone was in on a secret, apart from me.

'No, I'll see you soon. Just do as these men say, and be a good girl.'

With that, he turned and left the room. There was the resounding slam of the front door, and the men were still staring at me as Barry's car engine started up outside. I glanced through the window as he pulled to the top of the drive, indicated left and disappeared from view.

'Come on,' one of the men said, grabbing his jacket off the back of the sofa. 'We need to go.'

'Where are we going?' I asked.

'You'll see.'

The men led me to another car, parked outside, and told me to climb in. I didn't want to, but all of them were high – coked up – so I was scared what might happen if I refused. The car journey was silent so I stared out of the car window, wondering how I'd got myself in this situation. I had no clue where I was or where we were going; I didn't even know where Barry had gone off to. All I knew was now – right now – I had to do as these men asked, otherwise I might disappear entirely. I tried to quell the nausea and fear rising inside me. It was the first time since the prom that I hadn't felt in control, and that terrified me.

'Where are we going?' I asked again, but the men refused to answer.

A short while later, we pulled up outside a pub. I almost wept with happiness.

A drink. They're taking you for a drink!

But, as I climbed out of the car, one of the men pointed to a door on the corner, at the side of the pub.

'Inside and upstairs,' he grunted.

We reached the top of the stairs and the man beckoned me inside a flat. It was the biggest flat I'd ever been to. As soon as we walked in, I spotted lots of drugs scattered across a table. There was a girl I didn't know, and three white men inside. Without warning, two of the men and the girl left and the remaining man stood up and led me through into a bedroom. He was middle-aged, but he wore jeans and a shirt that were far too young for him. Inside the room was an old-style round, wooden dressing table, which had a large mirror perched on top. Someone had already lined up heaps of cocaine along its surface, waiting to be snorted. The man helped himself to the coke and then to me. I tried to pretend it wasn't me but someone else he was having sex with as I stared over at the dressing table until he'd finished. Afterwards, he calmly got up and dressed himself. I went to do the same.

'No, you wait.'

Moments later, another man appeared. This one was also middle-aged but he looked absolutely wasted. He pinned me down and raped me as I focused on the dressing table. The man finished, got up from the bed, and lined up more of the cocaine.

'You want some?'

I nodded. I needed it if I wanted to get through this. He wiped some white, tell-tale powder from his nose, got dressed and left me alone in the room. Laughter and Hawaiian-style music drifted up through the window from the pub downstairs. It reminded me of warm holidays and days out on the beach as my head swam and cocaine buzzed through my system. If I concentrated hard enough, I could almost smell the suntan cream and cocktails. Just feet below, everyone was having a great time – drinking and laughing. Everyone was enjoying themselves; everyone apart from me. Numb and disorientated, I glanced down at the floor and realised for the very first time it was bare – there was no carpet. The flat was a complete dive. Suddenly, the bedroom door creaked open a third time, and another man – also in his forties – entered the bedroom. By now I knew what I had to do, so I let him have sex with me, as the laughter and noise from the pub reached a crescendo.

By the time he'd finished with me I was buzzing with adrenalin from the coke. The last man got to his feet and told me to get dressed.

'There's a car coming to pick you up.'

As I stood, I realised the window overlooked the rest of the town. There was a parade of shops opposite, and I wondered how many people on the street below would guess there was a fifteen-year-old girl upstairs, having sex with countless men. As I stepped away from the window, I caught my reflection in the dressing-table mirror and barely recognised myself. My face was all flushed, my hair all messy and my eyeliner had smudged black down from my eyes to the top of my cheeks. I licked a finger and tried to rub the smudge marks away. As I did, I saw a child stare back at me and realised just how young I looked; a child playing at trying to be a grown-up. Although it wasn't a game, I was that child and I'd been caught up in a brutal world I didn't fully understand. With my make-up fixed, the last man led me back downstairs to wait for the car.

I'd hoped it might be Barry, coming to pick me up. The longer we waited, the harder I found it to concentrate because I was bursting for the toilet.

'I really need a wee!' I said, wriggling around, crossing my legs. 'Can I just nip back upstairs and use the toilet?'

The man refused.

'No, use the one in the pub.'

The bar had a beach theme and there were large plastic coconuts hanging down outside, swaying in the breeze. I wondered why I couldn't just nip up to the flat but the man was adamant I couldn't go back inside.

'Pub,' he ordered, nodding over at it.

But I was only a teenager and I was worried the landlord might throw me out.

'Will they let me?'

'There's some other stairs up to the toilet at the side. You don't have to go through the pub.'

I walked past the fake hanging coconuts, looking for the stairs. 'Club Tropicana' by Wham wafted underneath a side door as the man began to follow me. It was as though he didn't trust me and wouldn't let me out of his sight. I nipped to the ladies, but when I came out he was still standing there, waiting for me.

'Come on,' he said gruffly.

Soon we were back outside, but the car still hadn't appeared so I sat on one of the pub's low windowsills and lit

107

a cigarette. The cocaine I'd snorted had left my mouth as dry as sand. I felt odd and uncomfortable; the man didn't say a word to me even though we'd just had sex. Moments later, a black car pulled up – the same one that had taken me there. But Barry was nowhere to be seen. Instead, a young lad – around twenty – was sitting behind the steering wheel.

'In the back,' the older man ordered, holding open the door.

I was too afraid to argue so I did as he said.

To my utter relief I spotted another girl, who looked about the same age as me, sitting in the back seat. As I slid next to her, she glanced up before looking back down at the footwell. The girl had shoulder-length brown hair and a really pretty face.

'Hi,' I smiled.

She lifted her head slightly and smiled back.

'You okay?'

She shrugged her shoulders as though she didn't really know.

'Ssssuppose sssso,' she slurred, turning her face towards mine. Although she was young, her eyes were old as though she was already dead inside. It was obvious she'd been drugged up. The girl had a Brummie accent, and I was curious to know more about her.

'How old are you?'

'Ffffifteen,' she replied, trying to whisper so the driver wouldn't hear. 'I'mm ffffifteen but ...' her voice trailed off.

She inspected her fingers and began nervously picking at some loose skin. 'Th … th … the thing is … I think I'm pr … pr … pregnant.'

I was horrified; it was obvious this poor girl was being driven around to different houses to have sex with multiple men. How would she even know who the father was? I shuddered – that girl could have been me.

'What are you going to do about the baby?'

'Shut the fuck up! Stop talking! You're not allowed to talk to each other.'

It was the driver.

I glanced at the girl, but she refused to look at me after that. It was clear she was absolutely terrified. We drove for another half an hour before parking up outside another huge house. Unlike that last one, this place was way posher. But we didn't go through the front door; we walked in through the back and straight into the kitchen. It was massive, with a marble-topped island in the middle. But I didn't have much time to take it in because we were on the move.

'You!' the young lad said, pointing at me. 'You follow me.'

We passed a downstairs toilet and then entered a grand hallway. There were stairs on both sides, and a huge gilt-framed mirror that hung on the wall between them. There was one long staircase that turned to the left and another that twisted to the right.

'Not the left one, go up the right,' the lad insisted.

I nodded and proceeded to climb the stairs. There was a bedroom at the top, which he told me to go inside. As I did, he nipped through to the en-suite toilet. I wasn't sure what to do, so I followed him.

'Get back in the fucking room!'

I waited, wondering what had happened to the other girl.

Had she gone up the staircase on the right? I couldn't be sure. All I knew was she'd been there one minute, but not the next.

There was the sound of water running and realised the boy was having a shower. Moments later, he emerged wrapped in a towel.

'Here,' he said, throwing me a clean towel. 'Your turn.'

He was only young, but I felt perfectly safe. I'd suffered at the hands of much older men so he held no fear. Instead, I stripped off and washed myself clean of all the men who had had their hands all over my body. It felt good to wash them off me. Afterwards, I lay on the bed with the boy next to me; he was completely naked, but he didn't try anything on and I knew he wouldn't. He was just the messenger. It was really late – about three or four o'clock in the morning – so we slept until light flooded the room, waking us both.

I got out of bed and studied my reflection in the mirror, wondering how the hell I'd ended up there. The pregnant girl flashed through my mind.

Where did they take her?

Grabbing my handbag, I pulled out some make-up and tried to apply it but my hand was trembling. Then I heard the sound of car tyres crunch against the gravel driveway outside. It was Barry; he'd come back for me. My body flooded with relief. I gathered my stuff and ran outside.

'Get in,' Barry said, nodding to the passenger seat.

Throughout the journey I'd expected him to ask me what had happened or if I was okay, but he said nothing. And then it struck me: I wasn't just his drug mule any more, I'd become his teenage prostitute.

A few weeks later, not long after my sixteenth birthday, Barry drove me and Andrea to an Indian restaurant in the middle of the countryside in a picturesque Welsh town. There was a flat above the Indian with five men waiting inside. I recognised the men as friends of Mo's, but they didn't want sex; one pulled out a Polaroid camera and began to take naked photographs of us. They plied us with drugs and booze first, so we went along with it, thinking it was all a bit of a laugh. A few weeks later Barry picked me up again, only this time Carys came with me. We drove ten or so miles and pulled up outside another huge house. Inside were twenty men – a mixture of white and Pakistani Welsh – waiting to have sex. From the outside the house seemed nice and respectable – too respectable. I wondered if it had been rented just for this purpose.

One man approached me to ask something.

'Shall we have a threesome?'

The others jeered, egging him on.

I looked at Carys and shook my head. The man seemed disappointed, almost dejected, and then he shrugged.

'Well, if you don't ask, you don't get.'

That night I hadn't been feeling too good. I was on my period and the last thing I wanted was to be passed around as a sexual plaything between a group of disgusting blokes. I was just about to protest when two of them grabbed hold of me by my arms and dragged me upstairs.

'Get off me, you bastards. Carys …' I cried.

Just as I'd called her name, I heard Carys's screams echo mine and I knew they were doing the exact same thing to her.

In spite of my protests and the fact I was on my period the men – one white, the other Pakistani – pinned me down on a bed and raped me. Thankfully, if you could even call it a blessing, because I was on my period, word had reached the others downstairs who decided to leave me be. I'd cried that night down at the prom; I'd cried until I had no tears left. Afterwards, I never cried like that again. It was as though everything that followed could never be as brutal – no matter how bad – nothing could be worse than that night.

Over the year that followed, Barry pimped me out; it seemed as though I'd grown too old to be his drug mule. Instead, he'd found a different, more lucrative use for me.

With my new chaotic lifestyle, I began getting into trouble with the police – usually for anti-social behaviour. One day I was arrested and cautioned for setting off a fire alarm at college. I'd been high on drugs at the time and I just couldn't be bothered any more. Looking back, it had been a cry for help. I wanted to tell the police what I'd got myself caught up in, yet, no matter how hard I tried, I couldn't. Deep down, I was frightened of repercussions. I knew once I'd blown the whistle it would open up a huge can of worms. I was far too frightened of Barry and what he was capable of to cross him. Instead, the police would find me hanging around the streets and bring me back home, much to my parents' despair.

'I don't know what's got into you, Em, but this has to stop,' Dad shouted in the kitchen one night. My father had always been so laid back, yet my disruptive behaviour was beginning to test even his patience.

One day at college, Yvonne had asked me to do something in class.

But I was tired and hungover.

'Oh, why don't you just go fuck yourself!'

She was so furious that she grabbed hold of me by my hair. I tried to wrestle her off but soon realised there was no point – she was in a position of authority so, by default, would always win. Yvonne put me in her car and drove me back home.

'She's rude … and she's disruptive in class,' she told Mum, who shook her head in despair.

I stormed past them both and went upstairs. As I did, I could still hear Yvonne speaking to my mother.

'I'm really not sure we can cope with her behaviour much longer, Mrs Vaughn. She really needs to …'

Her voice faded to nothing as I slammed my bedroom door and left them to it.

Later that evening, Mum came to speak to me. She tentatively knocked at my door and asked if she could come in.

'Whatever this is,' she said, exasperated and holding out both hands, 'it needs to stop. And it needs to stop right now.'

I could tell she was thoroughly sick of me. I opened my mouth to say something; to tell her – to explain what had happened to her little girl – but no words would come.

'Right, I see. That's how it is. Well, this is my house, and you need to play by my rules, and that means not being dragged home by the police at every hour of the morning. Understand?'

I scowled.

'Emily, I'm talking to you. I said: do you understand?'

I shrugged petulantly.

Mum lifted a hand and cupped it against her ear. 'Sorry, I didn't catch that. What did you say?'

'Yes,' I mumbled.

'Good! So you need to buck your ideas up or move out.'

With that, she left. As the door slammed closed, I rolled my eyes towards the ceiling.

So I almost fainted when, only a few weeks later, I heard a knock at the front door.

'Hi, is it possible to speak to Emily Vaughn?'

Mum asked who she was and the woman explained she was a female detective. I scoured my brains, trying to remember what I'd done wrong.

What if the police had caught up with Barry? Maybe Ashley had cracked under pressure and bleated it all out about the drug runs?

Another thought crossed my mind and I cringed.

What if she knows about all the sex I've been having with different men for Barry? What will I say to Mum?

No, I decided, shaking my head as I went downstairs. Whatever she asked, I'd deny it all – every last bit. It'd be up to them to try and prove it.

'Can I get you a cup of tea?' Mum asked as she politely showed the detective through to the front room.

'No, no, I'm fine, thank you.'

As I opened the door and stepped into the room, the female police officer rose from her seat and put her hand out to greet me.

Am I in trouble? She wouldn't shake my hand if I was?

I returned a half-hearted smile and flopped down onto the sofa. Mum settled down next to me as we both looked over at the detective, trying to second-guess why she was there.

'Emily, I'd like to ask you a few questions … about Barry Smith.'

This is it, I thought as my heart pounded and my breath snagged inside my chest. I swallowed down my nerves and tried to arrange my face into a blank expression.

Don't flinch; don't give anything away.

I rested both palms flat against the knees of my jeans to cool them down. I hoped she wouldn't pick up on my flushed face or notice the nervous sweat as it prickled against my forehead – the guilt quite literally pouring out of me.

'Barry? What about him?' I replied, trying to sound surprised.

'Well, it's just that we have reason to believe that Barry Smith has acted inappropriately with an underage girl, and I wondered if he'd ever done anything or touched you in a way that made you feel uncomfortable?'

'Oh my God!' I heard Mum gasp. She clamped a horrified hand against her mouth. 'Not Barry! I mean, did he ever touch you, Emily? If he did, then you need to tell this lady … you need to …'

I turned towards Mum and felt the nervous breath I'd been holding inside come rushing out of my lungs in pure relief.

She didn't know anything; she didn't know about the drug runs or the other stuff.

I wanted to weep with joy, but I knew I had to compose myself and try to act casual.

Don't trip up, not now.

I pretended to consider her question: Barry had touched me when I was younger – only once – but he had.

The heat from his hand as he'd rested it on my inner thigh – the way his fingers had snaked up between my legs …

I shook my head; partly to rid myself of the memory but mainly for the benefit of the detective. All the blow jobs I'd given him flashed at the back of my mind. The way he'd sneered with delight whenever he'd got what he wanted. Barry always got what he wanted.

'No,' I replied firmly. 'He never laid a finger on me.'

The officer looked at me curiously as though trying to peer down into my soul.

'Are you sure? Are you absolutely certain that Barry Smith never touched you inappropriately?'

I nodded.

'Yes, I'm absolutely certain.'

Mum rested a relieved hand against her chest.

'Well, thank God for that! He was always taking Emily and Ashley – you know, his youngest step-daughter – out in the van. I'd never forgive myself if he'd done something to Em. Angela was right to throw him out. No wonder she did …'

If only she knew. I thought, before rising to my feet.

'Is that it? Can I go now?'

The detective smiled and nodded.

'Yes. Thank you, Emily.'

I went over towards the door and was just about to turn the handle when the detective stopped me in my tracks.

'But if I have any further questions then I'll have to come back; is that okay?'

I turned around and smiled.

'Sure; not a problem. Any time.'

Then I left the room; I couldn't get out of there fast enough.

My legs climbed the stairs – two at a time – as I ran to the safety of my bedroom. My heart was hammering so fast that I thought it would leap out. I slumped down on the edge of the bed and allowed my head and shoulders to flop down to my knees. I took a deep breath. The same scene played over and over again inside my brain; Barry's hand between my legs as we drove along the country lanes in his van. The vision of him lunging forward, trying to grab Beca as we'd sat on her mum's bed.

So, Barry had been a paedophile all along. I shook my head and counted my blessings; at least she'd not asked about the drug runs or sex gangs.

After that day I never saw Barry again. I felt relieved he'd gone. At least he wouldn't be able to pimp me out; not any more. But, as I was about to find out, the worst wasn't over; in fact, the worst was yet to come.

CHAPTER SEVEN

SELF-HARM

If I thought all my problems would vanish with Barry, then I was mistaken because, as I discovered to my cost, I replaced one destructive thing with another. During those early dark days and in the months and years that followed, Andrea introduced me to something to help my anxiety. It would ease the pain between all the sex, phetamine, weed and pills. Now I had a brand-new addiction – self-harm.

'Here, pass me your arm,' she demanded as we stood together in the college toilets. I pushed up my sleeve and offered my right to her.

She gripped the razor between her fingers and it hovered over my delicate skin, like a wasp about to strike.

She examined my arm with the skill of a doctor, turning it this way and that, trying to locate my major arteries.

'You need to cut it from your elbow to your wrist; that way, you can hide it underneath your sleeve. See,' she said.

She lifted up the sleeve of her jumper to show me a battlefield of scars running the length and breadth from her wrist upwards.

'How long have you been doing it?' I asked, trying not to let her see how shocked I was. There were so many of them, thin ones, some wider with more raised edges; ones more recent and fresher.

'Ever since I was raped by Phil.'

My heart felt like a lead weight hanging inside my chest as Andrea spoke of the rape.

'But what about your mum and dad? Didn't you tell them?'

I thought of her parents and how weird she'd said they were. They didn't seem like a very close family at all.

Andrea took a deep breath and shook her head.

'I didn't tell them, but I reported it to the police.'

'And what did they do?'

She shrugged her shoulders.

'That was it, you see. They didn't do a thing.'

'But why?'

Andrea lifted her thin face to look at me.

'I was fifteen when I was raped, but when I later reported it the police did nothing.'

I could see she was trying her best to try and hold it all together.

I wasn't close to my parents but I knew Mum, and I knew she'd kill anyone who'd harmed me. I wondered what she would think of me now, sleeping with all these different men. I decided I could never tell her; it would kill her. As for Dad, well, he'd probably go out, round them all up, and strangle them with his bare hands.

'That's when I started cutting myself,' she explained.

I leaned against the edge of the sink as I digested everything she'd told me.

'I've blocked a lot of it out. All I do know is it made me feel better and it'll make you feel better too.'

With that she looked back down at my exposed arm.

'You want me to do it, or do you want to do it yourself?'

'You. You do it for me,' I said, turning away. I couldn't bear to watch.

There was a stinging, burning pain, but a nice pain all the same as Andrea's bony fingers dragged the silver blade across the surface of my arm. It cut against soft skin as it drifted down, scoring my skin like a skater on ice. Heat of the burn rose as blood oozed from the edges of the crimson stripe.

The anxious breath I'd been holding inside came rushing out from my lungs.

'Better?' she asked.

I looked down at the deep cut along my arm and then back up at her.

'Yeah.'

Andrea explained she'd stolen the razor blade from her mother. She kept it tucked inside a metal tobacco tin, but would get it out and slice her arm whenever things became too much.

'It helps, and it'll make you feel better. Just use it when you need to, that way you'll control your own pain.'

But I was too frightened to cut my own arm at first; I constantly worried I'd cut myself too deep, or that I might slip with the razor.

'It's okay,' Andrea said. 'I'll cut you for the first week; show you how to do it until you get the hang of it.'

I felt grateful I had someone to look out for me. Sure enough, after a week of cutting my arms until they were awash with ribbons of red scars, Andrea handed her razor to me so I could do it myself. I still didn't feel super-confident but, with her expert guidance, I made the first long injury, steadily tracing the metal edge against my skin until it had seared and marked me.

'That's it!'

As the fire grew and the pain intensified, I knew things would feel better. I let out a strangulated breath. She was right; it was the only way to feel better; this, alcohol and drugs. By shredding my arms daily, it felt as though I was releasing the badness. A secret opening of flesh to release all the pent-up pain, fear and inadequacy I'd held inside. Once I'd started it was as though I'd turned on an emotional tap and now I couldn't turn it off again. Now I couldn't settle until I'd made myself bleed.

After that first cut, Andrea turned to me in the same way a teacher would turn to her pupil.

'I've brought you a present,' she said, lifting the lid off her baccy tin. She held it out in her hand so I could peer inside.

She parted the roll-ups to reveal a brand-new razor, lying on its side.

'I've brought you your own,' she said, taking it from the tin. She held it between her fingertips as though it was the crown jewels before placing it flat in the middle of my palm. 'There you go; it's yours to keep. Now we can do it together.'

I twisted my hand under the strip lighting of the toilet; the edge of the razor glinted as it caught the light.

'But where did you get it?'

She tapped the side of her nose as though it was a trade secret.

'Where I get everything – from my mum. She's a bloody hypochondriac so she brings home all sorts of things. Our house is like a bloody chemist! You should see the inside of the bathroom cabinet – there's boxes and boxes of pills. Anyway, it's yours to keep, but don't lose it, will you? I can only nick so many, otherwise she'll know it's me.'

I curled my fingers around my palm and the razor.

'Thanks, Andrea. I'll look after it; I promise.'

We began to compare arms weekly until it had turned into a competition of who had the worst scars. It became my new addiction.

A few weeks later, following a particularly frenzied fortnight of self-harm, I was sitting at the kitchen table, eating my dinner. I'd just put the fork to my mouth when Mum grabbed me and pushed my sleeve up to my elbow.

'What the …'

My heart jumped from my chest into my mouth as she tried to grab my other arm. My left was even worse than my right so I pulled it away defensively.

'Show me!' she demanded.

'No!'

My face flushed because I knew I'd been found out; Mum had just discovered my dirty little secret.

'Show me!' she asked a second time, standing up from the table.

Mum was absolutely furious; I'd never seen her in such a temper. I watched as she picked up a plate and smashed it hard against the floor. Shards of broken pottery skittered across the kitchen.

'Fucking show me!'

I shook my head and began to back away from her. She picked up a mug and threw it down against the ground.

SMASH!

It was as though she was trying to shock me; snap me back to my senses with the plates and her language.

'What's got into you lately? Why the fuck have you done that?' she demanded to know, pointing at my arm.

I pulled my sleeve down and tried to hide.

'Em, why have you done that thing to yourself? Why the fuck are you doing this? Is it college? Is it these new friends you're keeping? Tell me, because I haven't got a bloody clue what's gotten into you lately!'

But I didn't know what to say; how could I tell her I was sleeping with multiple men every week to fund my drug and alcohol habit? How could I explain the only way her little girl could feel better was to slash her arms in the bedroom night after night? How could I tell her any of it?

'So, are you going to tell me what this is all about?'

I shrugged; it made her worse. She picked up my plate.

SMASH.

'Tell me!'

She picked up her own.

SMASH!

'Tell me!'

She grabbed a glass.

SMASH!

But I couldn't; I couldn't explain why I did these things or why I felt so utterly worthless.

'You know what you are,' Mum said, on the verge of tears. 'You are nothing but a disappointment.'

Her words sliced into me much deeper than any razor. She stood there with tears in her eyes, searching my face, waiting for answers I couldn't give.

'Can I go now or do you want to smash some more stuff?' I shouted, sounding like a typical teenager – I couldn't help myself.

I ran up to my bedroom and threw myself down on the bed. Holding my jumper sleeves taut in each hand, I stayed that way so no one else would be able to see how I'd started to unravel, bit by bit.

I heard Mum talking on the phone to someone downstairs. I pressed my ear against my bedroom door to try and listen.

'Yes, it's for my daughter. Yes, it's urgent! A doctor, yes,' I heard her voice and fragmented answers.

A few moments later, there was a knock at my door.

'Em, listen, it's me. I'm sorry, Em; it's just that I'm really worried about you. Anyway, that was the doctor on the phone and she's asked me to bring you in so that she can have a chat with you. Is that okay? The doctor says she can see you tonight.'

My mind whirred; I felt emotionally spent and utterly exhausted.

What the hell would I say to the doctor? What if she saw through my lies? What if she knew about all my visits to the clinic to get the morning after pill? What if she already knew it all – the men I'd slept with, all the pregnancy tests I'd taken?

I began to shake until soon I couldn't stop.

No, I told myself. There's no way she would or could know all those things because they were confidential. Besides, I'd never given my real name or address. I rested a hand against my pounding heart to try and calm myself down. I was still safe, for now.

CHAPTER EIGHT

A DUTY OF CARE

'So tell me, Emily, in your own words, and you can take your time, there's no rush. How are you feeling?'

The doctor was kind and tried her best to find out what was wrong with me, but I just couldn't tell her. I couldn't tell anyone. I laced my fingers together in my lap and stared down at them. At least that way I wouldn't have to look up at her, or Mum.

'Go on, Em, tell the doctor. Tell her what's been going on,' Mum chipped in. 'I don't know what's wrong with her lately, Doctor. I'm worried sick.'

'I'm sure you are, Mrs Vaughn. Now, Emily,' the GP said, leaning towards me as though we were old friends. 'Your mum has told me you've been hurting yourself on your arms. Could you show me? Can I have a look?' she asked, peering over the top of her tortoiseshell glasses.

I shook my head, grabbed the cuffs of my jumper and pulled both sleeves down before anchoring the edges in my gripped fists.

'Okay,' she decided, looking over at Mum, sitting in the chair next to me. 'That's fine. You don't have to show me if you don't want to, but what I would like to know is why you do it. Tell me, Emily, why have you been cutting the skin on your arms?'

Emotion bubbled up inside me; it rose from my toes, up my legs, my stomach and into my chest to settle somewhere at the back of my throat. I choked it back down. I wanted to tell her, but how could I? If I told her why, then I'd have to tell her everything, and I couldn't do that. I couldn't tell anyone. Shame washed over me.

'It's college,' I suddenly blurted out, the words leaving my mouth before I'd even had the chance to think what I'd said.

The doctor rested back in her chair, turned to her keyboard, and began to type something into her computer.

'I see, and what is it about college that makes you do this?'

Mum straightened up against the back of her chair; I could tell that she was finding this as excruciating as I was.

'I'm struggling. I'm struggling with my work.'

I couldn't tell her what had really been happening; my secret was far too big to share, plus, with Mum in the room, it felt too awkward to speak the truth, even a half-truth.

'Right, I see,' the doctor mumbled, continuing to type.

But I knew she didn't see. Not really; she didn't have a clue. No one did. Only Andrea knew what it felt like to be me.

'And is there anyone you could talk to? One of the lecturers?'

'It's not just my work,' I sighed, looking up and then

back down at my lap. I started to pick at a stray hangnail on my finger. 'It's everything. My friendships – everything. I just feel so overwhelmed.'

It was true; I did feel overwhelmed, just not for those reasons. I wanted to tell them, I really did, but I couldn't. The possible repercussions terrified me. If I told them then they'd want to know where I got my drugs from and who these men were; I didn't even know half of their names. As for the drugs, I was certain if I did tell then one of Barry's friends would make me pay.

The doctor pulled out some leaflets and addressed Mum rather than me.

'I'm going to refer Emily to CAMHS – it's a child and adolescent mental health service provided by the NHS,' she said, passing her one of the leaflets. 'They have trained counsellors and specialists there who I'm sure would be able to help Emily.'

My mum began to flick through the leaflet as the doctor typed up the last of her notes. With the appointment over, we both stood up while Mum thanked the doctor for seeing me at such short notice. It was only when we got home that her questions started.

'I thought you were happy at that college. You know you can talk to me any time, don't you, Em?'

Her questions made me feel claustrophobic. I could barely stand to be in the same house now that she knew. I felt stupid; humiliated that she'd seen my scars – the same scars I'd shown with pride to Andrea.

Days later, a letter fell through the letterbox onto the doormat at home. It was from CAMHS, informing me there was a long waiting list. In the end, I waited from February until August to get an initial appointment. Until that time I continued to have sex with multiple men for drugs and alcohol. That was my life now, and I just couldn't seem to break the cycle.

I attended my first CAMHS appointment on my own – it was part of the arrangement. The thinking was if I went alone I'd feel able to talk more freely without Mum breathing down my neck. But, in fact, the opposite happened because I knew anything I said in those meetings would be confidential. They wouldn't tell my parents anything, so I took full advantage. Often, my counsellor would come to our house and Mum would leave. We'd sit in the living room and she'd give me fags. Although she skirted around the issue of my self-harm, we never actually ever spoke directly about it. Instead, we'd talk about random stuff – the weather, music, clothes and how college was going. I knew everyone thought I was depressed, and maybe I was. But I convinced myself that I was having the time of my life with the drugs, men and my new crazy friends. I was living life on the edge and, in many ways, I felt alive. Sometimes, when I was at college, I'd have to call at the Children's Centre for sessions. By this point I was past caring and would often turn up for appointments drunk or high from smoking dope. Andrea or Stacey would drop me off and wait outside for me, but they were usually as stoned or pissed as I was. I tried to convince myself there was nothing wrong with my life; it was exciting. However, once the drugs and alcohol wore off and the hangover began to kick in, I'd feel even lower.

My counsellor was convinced I was a teenage rebel when actually my drugs, alcohol use and self-harm were there to anaesthetise myself against the rest of the world. It wasn't that I didn't like my counsellor; I just didn't see the point of 'talking things through'. Even my taste in music had changed. I'd progressed from chart music to black ghetto music. I pinned up Tupac posters on my bedroom walls and became immersed in rap music where women were seen as disposable sex objects. In short, Tupac's lyrics seemed to echo my life. I put up other posters with the words slag, slut and hardcore. It was what we'd been labelled by these men and so I wore it as a badge of honour. I'd begun to dress and do my hair that way too. It had become ingrained in my whole attitude to life and soon there was no escape. I'd fallen into this world and now I couldn't find a way out of it.

I'd become good mates with Bronwyn, who was in the same class as me at college. Bronwyn's mum was dating a Turkish man called Yusuf who owned a kebab shop in a village about twenty minutes' drive from our town. Mo was friends with Yusuf, so I felt as though we were already connected through friends. In spite of my time at the prom with Mo, I had grown to like and trust him. As long as I gave him what he wanted then he would keep me supplied with free food, drugs and drink.

One day, Bron asked if I wanted to go to a village inland with her neighbours Rhys and Dylan. There was a kebab takeaway that had a bedsit situated around the back. Yusuf drove us over and parked up outside the takeaway.

'Right, you girls go around the back. I've a few friends waiting to meet you.'

We knew what he meant by 'friends' but I didn't care. I was so far gone on pills that I felt I could take on the world. Sleeping with unknown men had effectively become my job. Once I'd accepted it, which I had, I knew I could live with it. Besides, I didn't feel I had another choice, not any more. It was too late.

Bron and I walked around the back of the takeaway. There was an alleyway next to a learner drivers' theory testing centre and then a dozen steps to climb. We strolled along to a corner, turned left, and the door was there right in front of us. We opened it to find a bedsit packed with half a dozen men. They were sitting there smoking weed and doing pills and phetamine bombs. The bombs were amphetamine wrapped in paper so when you swallowed one you would get an immediate buzz. I glanced down to my left and noticed a girl who only looked about fifteen. She was either sleeping or had passed out on the floor. The teenager was only half-dressed and was wearing a khaki-green-coloured mini-tube skirt that had been lifted up to her waist. Her hair was dark brown and long, but it had all matted at the back into a series of knots as though it hadn't seen a brush in ages. Apart from her skirt and knickers, her body was naked from the waist up. The bedsit windows had been covered with sheets that had been fastened, using nails hammered into wooden frames. The more I glanced around, the more I realised what a doss house it was. The whole flat was cold, damp and filthy – the kind of place you'd shudder if you saw it on television; it certainly wasn't a place a sixteen-year-old girl should be hanging around. My eyes scanned the men; they were sitting on grubby armchairs and a knackered old sofa, and that's when I realised – this was my new normal; this was what my life had become. We were there to do a job – have sex – and they wouldn't let us leave until we had. A man approached and led me over to a corner where I had sex with three men. Afterwards, Yusuf walked in and I witnessed money exchange hands. He'd just been paid for what me and Bron – his girlfriend's daughter – had done. All I received was a packet of fags and a bottle of poppers. Pressing my fingers against the top, I broke it off and sniffed hard; my head began to swim and my brain felt all fuzzy as though someone had taken life and smoothed over the rough edges. I'd never had poppers before, but afterwards I began to take them regularly along with anything else I could lay my hands on.

One day Bron asked if I wanted to go away for a few days with her, Yusuf and her neighbours Rhys and Dylan.

'Oh, and Andrea's coming as well,' she added.

I tried to hide my surprise. It was no secret that Andrea and Bron didn't get on, but I was happy that they seemed to be patching things up.

'Sure. I'll come. I'll just tell Mum I'm staying at yours, Bron.'

'Great!'

But, if I thought things were bad then, I didn't have a clue what was waiting for us just around the corner.

CHAPTER NINE

TELFORD

'So,' I said, taking a long drag of my fag as we sat in the back of Yusuf's car. 'Where is it we're going?'

'Telford. That's right, isn't it?' Bron asked Yusuf, tapping him on the shoulder as he concentrated on the road ahead.

'Yeah!'

'Telford,' Bron said, nodding at me. 'Told you.'

I laughed, but was still none the wiser.

'Never heard of it. Where's it near?'

'It's in England,' Rhys said, butting in.

'And what's it like?'

He shrugged.

'Just like every other shitty English town.'

We all burst out laughing.

'It's not Wales now, is it?' he added.

He was right; nothing compared. We were all Welsh and proud of it.

It turned out that Telford was near Shrewsbury, on the other side of the Welsh border.

'So, where are we going to stay?' I asked Yusuf as we drove into the outskirts of the town.

'Don't worry about that. I've got a mate who owns a place over there.'

He didn't need to elaborate because I knew what he meant; we'd be staying in another doss house, sleeping with men for money that he would keep. Only, it would be me and Bron doing all the work because Andrea had cried off at the last minute.

We pulled up in a car park that had been turned into an unofficial racing track. Engines roared as men raced each other in souped-up sports cars around a dirt track to show off their skills and their motors. I was introduced to a guy called Hussain, from Birmingham. In fact there were loads of men from Birmingham, who were a mixture of Chinese, Pakistani and white.

'Hey,' Yusuf said, greeting them as though they were old friends.

'Hey, bro,' Hussain called.

The race track was a bit dull, with lots of lads showing off, and the more ridiculous the alloys, spoilers or UV lights, the bigger the cheer. Soon it had started to grow dark, so Bron and I went to a nearby bingo hall to try and warm up. She seemed to know the area, so I presumed she must have been there before. After a while Bron turned to me.

'You hungry, Em?'

I nodded. It had been a long day – we'd left Wales at six o'clock that morning – and now it was evening. I was absolutely ravenous.

'Come on, follow me.'

Bron and I walked along the road towards a chippy, where we bought ourselves a bag each. I was still enjoying my chips when she started to hurry me up.

'What's the rush?' I asked.

'Doesn't matter; here, bring them and follow me.'

We strolled around a nearby corner and sat down on some green steps outside a newsagent's shop. But Bron still seemed distracted as I finished off my chips.

'Here he is,' she said, grinning, and stood up as Hussain approached.

'Allright, girls. You two ready?'

Even though I was full, my stomach fell away because it was time to do what we'd been brought here to do. Hussain led us up the green steps and towards a bedsit that was situated above the row of shops. With my chips all gone, I threw my empty wrapper on the ground. As we approached the door I noticed a flash of light and four figures in silhouette as they left the building. They pushed past with their heads still down, but I could tell, even in the dim light, that they were a group of four girls who didn't look much older than fourteen or fifteen years old. I tried to make eye contact with one, but she refused to look at me. Instead, the group rushed past as though they couldn't wait to get out of there.

'Come on,' Hussain said, ignoring the girls and pushing the door open.

Stepping inside, the first thing I noticed were men – nine or ten of them. Some were standing while others were seated; I did a quick head count – there were four sitting on the sofa alone. The other thing that hit me was the colour – everything was green; the walls, the carpet, even the settee. There were two single mattresses on the floor in two separate bedrooms off the main room, but I could hardly see them for the men, who were hovering inside both doorways. Someone offered us drinks.

'Yeah, I'll have vodka and Ribena,' I said, trying to sound super-confident.

I knew it would numb me and blur the edges. Bron and I smoked a couple of spliffs to try and chill. Once we were anaesthetised, the men suddenly became extremely organised. One took me off into a bedroom while Bron stayed in the front room. She'd already taken a handful of pills and was gurning as one of the men pulled me from the room. The others just sat there laughing at her. I heard Bron cry out as they grabbed and helped themselves to her. The bedroom I was in had two single beds that had been pushed together. The blue and orange mattresses were both ancient and there were no sheets covering them. As soon as I lay down I could feel sharp, metal springs digging into my back and thighs. But I was high on pills, so I couldn't protest or even try and fight them off as one of the men held me down and raped me. My back was pinned against the broken, old mattress as they then took it in turns. At one point I was in so much pain that my insides began to swell from internal friction burns. In a second I was back there – at the prom. Moving my arms, I tried to struggle because the pain had grown so intense; even the pills and weed hadn't been enough to numb it. It felt as though I was on fire between my legs. I tried to stand up but someone pushed me back down. I clambered to my feet but another hand reached out and grabbed my head; somehow, my hair became tangled in the metal links of his watch strap and it ripped from my scalp as he threw me back onto the filthy mattress.

'Argghhh!'

But the men didn't care. It was all part of the fun. It was a well-known fact that some men would even use ice-cubes to numb girls before vaginal and anal rape so that they didn't scream as much. That night I was raped by five men and Bron was raped by the rest. When they'd finally finished I tried to stand up but my legs gave way beneath me. I was in so much pain that I felt nauseous. My nostrils flared and I had to stop myself from throwing up because the flat smelled of hot bodies, sex and spices. Just when I thought my ordeal was over, some more men piled in from the bedsit next door and I was raped over and over again. It was relentless. I still have no idea how many guys raped me because there had been a constant flow coming in through the bedroom door. Fresh blokes meant more sex. It didn't matter that I was sore, battered and bruised. They didn't care. Instead, I overheard discussions between them: £20 for full intercourse, £10 for a blow job. Then Yusuf appeared. I spotted him through the crack in the half-opened door and watched as men handed him £10 and £20 notes, his fingers shuffling quickly as he totted up that evening's takings. Afterwards, once all the men had been satisfied and had left, Yusuf peeled off two £5 notes and handed us one each.

'There you go, girls. Go and buy yourself something.'

Bron grinned and pulled me by the arm.

'Come on, Em, let's go and get something.'

I felt her tugging the sleeve of my jumper, but my eyes were still on Yusuf. I knew how much money he'd just taken; I'd seen him counting the notes, yet £5 each was all he thought we were worth. But I was in a strange town with a man I barely knew. Bron was there, but we were effectively trapped because no one, apart from Rhys, Dylan and Andrea, knew we were in Telford.

'Come on, hurry up!' Bron nagged, still pulling at me to go.

Reluctantly, I grabbed my coat and followed her out of the door, down the steps and towards the centre of town.

My body burned with each step I took and I wondered if I'd ever feel normal again. But I knew I would heal as I'd healed time after time before. Sex had felt like any other bodily function and I'd trained my brain to separate from it when I was being raped. I'd be there in body, not in mind. There was no emotion or love attached to sex – it was just something I had to do, like going to the loo. Nothing more, nothing less.

Bron and I pooled our money together and spent £10 on blue slushes and a pack of ten fags.

'Let's get some chewing gum, too. I've got cotton mouth.'

Cotton mouth was common after taking too many pills and smoking too much weed. There was also a disgusting taste of semen inside my mouth. It'd felt as though someone had poured acid between my legs, but I'd grown accustomed to it – my pain threshold had increased. However bad I felt, I knew nothing could ever hurt as much as that first time at the prom, when I'd been ripped apart by dogs.

Yusuf was making money out of us and I should have cared, but I didn't because I felt worthless anyway.

Who would want you now?

I'd become soiled goods.

No one will ever want you. No one.

None of it mattered. As long as Yusuf kept me topped up with vodka, pills and drugs then I knew I'd do pretty much anything. I was addicted and I'd become dependent on it and on those who fed it to me. I'd been groomed for years – since the age of eleven. It'd started with Barry and soon one thing had replaced another – a carousel of pain, rape and addiction. This had become my life, whether I liked it or not.

CHAPTER TEN

THE FOOTBALL CLUB

We'd started hanging around a football club during our lunch breaks from college. I can't even remember why we'd first started going there, but one of the girls from class knew the guy who ran it. He was called Dox and one day he asked if we would wash his car, which he parked next to the football pitch, behind the goals.

'What's in it for us?' Andrea asked cheekily.

Dox looked up at us, a hand shielding his eyes from the sun.

'I'll tell you what; you girls do a good job on my car and you can go around the other side of the bar and help yourselves.'

'Deal!' we all agreed.

That day we washed his car until it was sparkling clean.

'A deal's a deal.' He nodded approvingly. 'You know where the bar is.'

With that, we all dashed inside to drink as much booze as we could before going back to our lessons. However, as I discovered, there is no such thing as a free drink, and soon Dox started to demand sex from us all along with his mate,

Colin. I knew Dox wasn't to be trusted because it was common knowledge that he liked to have sex with school-girls – some as young as fourteen. But we decided that as long as he kept us supplied with booze and fags then we wouldn't rock the boat. Then creepy Colin asked if we'd have a threesome with him.

'Not a chance!' I insisted.

But Andrea agreed, and so did another girl, so he not only got his way, he filmed it. Colin liked to film everything. It was still the early days of mobile phones, so he had a removable SIM card that he would fill with sleazy film footage. Looking back, he probably downloaded it straight onto his computer, but it's something we'll never know. All I did know was Colin constantly stood there – his phone in his hand and flipped to one side – and filmed us all having sex.

'He gives me the creeps,' I remarked to Andrea, who came up with a plan to get our own back.

Dox started to invite other men to join in with our sex sessions. They came from everywhere, Oxford, Telford, Birmingham and Blackpool. In fact, I became so talented at recognising regional accents that I could immediately tell where someone came from as soon as they opened their mouth. Soon, word had spread, and there would be up to fifteen teenage girls at any one time, sleeping with a room of thirty different men. The men were all ages and colours – white, black and Asian. The abuse had nothing to do with the colour of their skin because all of them seem to prefer sex with girls barely out of puberty. Whenever there wasn't a function or event being held, the football club would become a den of iniquity. It'd look like a scene from a Roman orgy, with bodies writhing everywhere, from the back rooms, across rows of seats and even on the floor. Dox would put out blankets for those who preferred to protect their modesty when getting frisky with young girls. Others didn't care who saw what and would demand full or oral sex in full view. Among those from Birmingham, Blackpool and Oxford, I also heard Welsh and Bristolian accents. It was a free-for-all – a sex party on an industrial scale – and they travelled from all over the country just to molest young girls.

There was a local taxi driver called Gary who gave us free lifts in return for a blow or hand job, even though he was supposedly happily married. Gary was good mates with Dox and creepy Colin, but I never had full sex with him. At almost fifty years old, he seemed ancient to a girl like me; besides he was fat and, because he pretty much lived in his car, he always smelled of body odour. One day Gary told me Tony – the man I'd delivered dodgy DVDs for on our estate – had wanted to see me.

'But he lives miles away, Gaz,' I replied, lighting up a cigarette.

It was true; Tony lived miles inland and on one of the roughest estates in Wales.

'No worries, I'll run you over there. Be a day out, if nothing else.'

I shrugged and looked at Andrea, Stacey and Marsha, who was still only thirteen.

'What do ya think?'

Andrea smiled and Stacey nodded. But Marsha was young and unsure so she stayed quiet.

'Yeah, I'm up for it, if you are?' Andrea agreed.

'Great!' Gary said, butting in. 'Get in the car then and I'll take you over now.'

I held up the cigarette between my fingers.

'But I've only just lit this?'

'Bring it. Get in; you can smoke it on the way!'

Half an hour later we'd pulled up outside Tony's flat. The area was rough; I knew it well because I'd run drugs there years before with Barry.

'Em! Good to see you,' Tony said, greeting me as though I was his best friend.

'Allright, Tony. What's all this then? Why did you want to see me?'

'You want some stuff?'

By stuff, I knew exactly what he meant – pills and weed.

'Sure,' I replied with a grin.

A short while later, after handing me a mixture of both, Tony got up to his feet.

'Come on,' he said, grabbing his jacket from a nearby chair. 'There's a friend of mine I'd like you to meet.'

Tony took me and Andrea to a house on another nearby estate. He knocked at a random door and a Pakistani man answered. I thought I recognised him from somewhere but couldn't remember where. It soon became obvious the man was expecting sex and I realised that Tony had set it and us up. Suddenly, more men appeared. By this point I was off my head on weed and pills so the rest of the afternoon was a bit hazy. In my drug-addled state Andrea seemed to come and then go; I'm certain she went into other houses on the estate, although I had no idea why. I spent most of the time pinned to a bed so that faceless men could rape me. I was still only young but, by now, I knew this wasn't sex but rape because I hadn't given consent. These men were using and abusing me for their own pleasure and others were exploiting and making money out of both it and me. Rape or not, sex wasn't a big deal to me any more. In fact, I felt numb whenever a man raped me. I felt nothing. I had become as unfeeling and dead as a lump of wood. In some respects I saw it as a good thing. If I couldn't feel anything then it almost didn't count.

Afterwards, we returned to Tony's flat, where we found another ten men waiting. I was absolutely exhausted and I didn't want to, but Tony had tricked us. He'd arranged for these guys, who were white and Chinese, to come over and have sex with us all, even thirteen-year-old Marsha. Tony had organised a sex party and we were the entertainment. He realised we weren't happy so he plied us with more booze and pills before organising us into a single line. The men sat opposite and – one by one – got up to choose which one they wanted to have sex with. I staggered as I was led upstairs by one man. On the way up I glanced out of the window and into the back garden. There was a scrub of grass that was bald in places, and a child's bike. It looked as if it belonged to a small boy and it was leaning against a wooden fence. The bedroom walls had been painted bright blue and red, and the bed was small, as though it belonged to a toddler. I spotted something on the floor, pushed underneath, and realised they were shoes – a little boy's shoes. The man threw me onto the bed, and the room drifted in and out of my consciousness as though the walls were flexing and bending in on me. The small, wooden bed felt cramped. I decided that it must belong to Tony's son. He had a wife and child, yet he was doing this in his own house with young girls. I wondered where his wife and son were.

Maybe they were away for the weekend? Maybe he'd waved them off, his wife totally unaware what her husband got up to when she wasn't at home.

Nothing shocked or surprised me any more.

After all the men had been satisfied, Gary drove us back home as though we'd all been on a jolly day out. It had been anything but. We'd been tricked, drugged and raped – all of us, even thirteen-year-old Marsha. I felt guilty; if she hadn't been with us, if only I hadn't agreed to go, then none of it would have happened. The thought of it continued to torture me.

* * *

Mo was also involved with the football club because he was friends with Dox and Colin. There was another man who also went there; he called himself The Stallion and he really fancied himself. The man, who was in his fifties, was tall and thin with brown hair that he wore slicked back. The Stallion saw himself as a bit of a ladies' man and dressed as though he was twenty years younger than he actually was.

'All right, Em,' he said, giving me a wink, as he pushed past me in the football club one night.

I felt my stomach turn. The others were repulsive, but The Stallion was as repulsive as creepy Colin.

Just then, Andrea nudged me and gestured over towards Colin, who was otherwise engaged – busy filming our friends having sex with one of the visiting men.

'I think he's filmed me and Sue on that phone having a threesome,' she whispered. 'I'm not happy, Em, and I'm going to get it back.'

'How?'

'Watch this.'

I stood there as Andrea went over to speak to another girl, who she'd obviously already primed. The girl managed to distract Colin, pretending she was interested in him, while Andrea ejected the SIM card from his phone and put the mobile back on a nearby table. She took the card and slipped it inside her bra.

'Hey, where's my phone?' Colin asked suddenly, looking up and patting the pockets of his jeans.

'Is this it?' Andrea asked innocently, pointing to the table.

Colin grinned, revealing a set of brown, tobacco-stained teeth.

'Yeah, thanks. I thought I'd lost it for a minute!'

Andrea turned and winked at me and I had to walk away because I was pissing myself laughing. We disappeared before Colin realised his SIM card was missing.

'So, where are you going to keep it?' I asked as we walked along a nearby street.

'I dunno. I can't keep it at home in case my parents find it.'

We looked all around us, and that's when she spotted something.

'Quick, Em. Over here.'

Andrea crossed the road and stopped by someone's garden.

'I'm going to hide it in there,' she said, pointing. I followed her finger towards a bird box, hanging from the branch of a nearby tree.

'Someone might see you!' I gasped, but it was too late. She'd already pushed the black SIM card inside it.

'There,' she said, wiping her hands against her jeans. 'Creepy Colin will never see that again.'

I linked my arm through hers as we strolled along the street laughing. It was only a small victory, but a victory all the same. Of course, Colin went mad when he later discovered it had gone missing. He'd stored all his favourite homemade porn movies on it. I'm sure that he must've had footage of us all, but Andrea had taught him a lesson. There would be no more amateur porn movies for creepy Colin. However, The Stallion continued to pester us for threesomes – it's all he ever seemed to want. We would go down the football club regularly and be given free drinks and fags, but there was always a price – sex.

One evening, not long after we'd first started going there, I'd walked down to the prom with Andrea and a few other girls. We were standing, smoking, chatting and listening to the roar of the waves when a girl we knew – Ellie – came running out of the shadows. She was crying and shaking uncontrollably. Ellie was only young but had mascara streaming down her face. She was sobbing so much that it was hard to try and make sense of what was wrong, or why she was crying.

'It's him; he did it to me,' she wailed.

I put my arm around Ellie to try and calm her, as Andrea asked her questions.

'Who? Ellie? Who are you talking about and what did he do?'

But she was so distraught that she could barely speak. Her whole body was racked with sobs and she tried her best to catch her breath so that she could tell us.

'Stallion. The Stallion,' Ellie blurted out while sobbing. 'He's just … he's just … raped me. Over there!'

Ellie pointed to the back of a building. Suddenly everything came racing back to me at breakneck speed.

The night at the prom; men's hands pawing my body, ripping off my clothes … *the mud on my trousers … blood in my knickers … the bite mark at the top of my breast …*

Silence was broken by laughter – Andrea's. She smirked at the rest of the group to try and get them to join in with her. Soon everyone was laughing, everyone apart from Ellie. She'd been brutally raped, and I knew what that felt like.

'Stop it,' I pleaded with Andrea, but she wouldn't listen. She didn't care about Ellie or anyone else.

'The Stallion. That sad old git? The Stallion raped you? Ha ha, ha ha …' she said, taking the piss.

I felt utterly nauseous. I hated Andrea in that moment – I hated them all, apart from poor, gentle Ellie. But however angry I felt, I knew I couldn't go against the others – it would be social suicide. Ellie looked devastated as I began to laugh along with the rest of the group. Like a total coward, I laughed even though deep inside I felt a piece of my soul break away.

I knew that I shouldn't have done it, but I'd become so deeply ingrained in this new way of life that to go against it would leave me an outcast, not only from this group, but from my whole social circle. Instead, I continued to laugh and to mock, even though it wasn't just wrong, it was disgusting. I'd been in the exact same place as Ellie at four-teen. She was two years older than I'd been yet no one had helped me. It had been a brutal lesson in life and one that had prepared me for what was about to follow. That evening, I felt ashamed of what I'd become, laughing at someone else's misfortune. I realised that I didn't even like myself, not any more.

CHAPTER ELEVEN

DERELICT FLATS

Yusuf would drive but stop off en route to Telford at a takeaway, where we'd be expected to have sex with men for money that he always kept. There would be ten, sometimes fifteen, Chinese men waiting every time we called; it was as though we'd become the actual takeaway. Some would use protection, but lots of others wouldn't. Naively, I didn't worry because I'd finally gone on the pill, so I knew I wouldn't get pregnant. Astonishingly, sexually transmitted infections never occurred to me. Once all the men had been satisfied, Yusuf would drive us over to the derelict flats. We'd climb the stairs and disappear off into different flats, where there'd be both white and Asian men waiting to have sex. The flats were ready to be demolished; most didn't even have running water, never mind electricity or heating. There was no furniture or even carpet, and a few of the properties had floorboards missing. As a result, we would have to have sex carefully, upon broken floors. Other girls went there, too, although it was an unwritten rule that it was the place to go for men who wanted to have sex with young and underage girls.

One day, Yusuf had taken me and Bron. We were just walking towards the concrete steps, which ran up at the side of the block, when a stream of twenty young girls emerged. I heard Birmingham and Telford accents as they passed yet not one of them made eye contact. None of the girls were allowed to speak to each other – it was another unwritten rule. We all knew what we were there to do.

Different drug dealers would travel over the border into Wales on the search for drugs – the country was rife with them – but it seemed we were part of the same bargain. The dealers would buy drugs from Wales and then traffic girls over to Telford to work alongside their own. In total, I visited Telford three or four times a week over five months. I was still only sixteen years old and barely at the legal age for consensual sex; yet here I was being raped by multiple men almost every night. There wasn't just one ethnicity. We were raped by black, Pakistani and white men, who would call us names such as whitey bitch, whitey slag, whitey whore. I'd already heard them all so it was like water off a duck's back. It was as though I'd built an internal metal shield to protect my emotions. There was nothing anyone could say or do to penetrate it because I was so numb with booze and drugs – nothing could touch me. However, just as I'd started to believe I was invincible, something strange happened. I don't know if it'd been all the oral sex I'd been forced to give, but I suddenly started to gag whenever I ate food. It was as though the act of putting something – anything –

inside my mouth made me want to vomit. I'd always been slim – around a healthy size 12 – but the weight began to fall off me until soon even a size 6 hung loosely off my body. Each time I put a morsel of food inside my mouth I felt as though I would choke. To try and beat it, I'd chew my food as best I could before spitting it out into a tissue. However, if I thought my new skeletal frame might put men off wanting to have sex with me, then I was wrong. If anything, they seemed to crave me even more. It was as though my 'prepubescent' body turned them on, especially in the derelict flats of Telford.

The doors to the flats in Telford often didn't shut because they'd been broken. Some were barely even there; instead, they'd hang off their hinges, giving a view to the occupants inside. It'd reached a point where I began to recognise the faces of some of the girls. After a long day, we'd often stay overnight because it was over an hour's drive to get back home to Wales. We'd sleep rough on bare or broken floorboards, or sit up all night, smoking and drinking until sunrise. It was after a particularly long night that I was threatened by a man with a knife. We'd been sitting in a car on our way back from Telford, when I got talking to a lad called David. Andrea said he'd wanted to marry her, so I sat there, taking the piss.

'So you're her boyfriend, are you? What? You're ugly and you're like thirty or something!'

Suddenly, David pulled the car over; the tyres screeched to a halt.

'See this road, yeah?' he said, pointing at it through the windscreen.

I smiled insolently and wondered where this was leading.

'It's haunted, and I'm going to leave you here.'

Without warning, the atmosphere changed as David snapped. He climbed out of the driver's seat and dragged me out of the car. I presumed he was going to abandon me at the side of the road, but then he pulled out a flick knife. I was still at the side of the car as he approached and held the blade against my throat. His eyes were wide and his face crimson with anger. He was so furious that he spat out words through gritted teeth. My heart hammered furiously because I was certain he would stab me.

'Think you're funny, do you?' he hissed, spittle flying everywhere. 'You think this is all a laugh? Well, it isn't. Go on, say it again; take the piss again and let's see what happens.'

I could barely breathe because I was so frightened. I'd hoped Andrea or one of the others might jump out and intervene, but no one dared say a word because everyone could see he'd totally lost the plot.

'I'm going to fucking kill you!' he screamed inches from my face. 'You hear me?'

Spittle showered my face as I flinched beneath him and the knife. My whole body was on full alert because he seemed so unpredictable – as though he was capable of anything.

'Understand?' he screamed again. The edge of the blade bit against the thin skin of my throat.

My eyes were wide with fear as I nodded. David shoved me hard against the side of the car in one last warning, his temper finally beginning to subside. Once he'd let go, I ran over to the grassy embankment to try and catch my breath. My hands searched for my mobile phone and were still trembling as I dialled 999. However, as soon as the call handler heard my Welsh accent and asked me where I was from, their tone changed.

'You need to ring your local station,' they unhelpfully informed me.

I was in the middle of nowhere and I didn't have a clue where the nearest local station was.

'You can stay here,' David barked over at me, as he climbed back into the passenger seat.

I wasn't sure quite what to do, but I didn't want to be abandoned in the middle of nowhere on my own. Sheepishly, I put my mobile away and walked over towards the car. I slid along the back seat and sat there – as quiet and as timid as a church mouse – till we'd reached home. I'd learned my lesson that day – these men weren't to be messed with.

Not long afterwards, the police raided the Telford flats and they were eventually boarded up by the council. They were demolished to build a new road, which put a stop to all our Telford trips. Relief washed over me – it was one less thing to have to face. However, Yusuf was still determined to make money. Instead, he'd drive us over to the takeaway flats – both Chinese and Indian – where we would have sex with the workers. Telford had come to a natural end, but I still recognised the familiar faces of young girls who then started being trafficked over to Wales. No one ever spoke about the derelict flats or mentioned Telford again.

CHAPTER TWELVE

BLACKPOOL

When Carys asked me if I wanted to go to Blackpool for the weekend, I knew it wouldn't be for the sun and sand, but for sex. Yusuf packed us into his car and drove us over to meet a bloke called Jason, who we knew from the football club but who also lived in Blackpool. Just off the seafront there was a pub where Yusuf dropped us off to meet Jason and his mates. They were already there, waiting inside for us. After a drink in the pub, we walked down towards a car park where we bought some Thai weed and sticky phetamine. By now, phet had become my drug of choice. With the drugs safely stashed inside our pockets, Jason drove us into Blackpool. There were seven of us crammed into his tiny car and I was worried we'd get pulled over – not for drugs, but because none of us were wearing seatbelts. We drove over to a flat where there were another twenty to thirty men waiting. I'd already told Mum I'd be staying at Carys's house that night, so she had no idea I was actually in another seaside town, miles away from home, with dozens of strange men. I felt safe because, not only did I have Carys with me, I also had my brand new

Nokia phone. It was the size of a brick, and as heavy, but I thought it would offer me an extra layer of protection – that I'd be able to call for help should we need it.

There was a mixture of white and Asian men inside the flat, which was situated opposite a car park. There was a long corridor with different rooms leading off it and both men and girls were milling about, smoking weed; the air was thick with it and the place stank of skunk. I was led into a small room that had two double beds crammed inside and very little else. One by one, eight different men pinned me down on the bed and raped me. There were other men, who watched as they masturbated. I felt ill, watching them watching me. It was as if I was the main star in a warped porn film or cheap peep show – only one without men hidden behind a wall. The sex went on for a couple of hours but, although I felt sore, my body had become used to the pain. Afterwards, Carys, I and some of the men strolled down to a local kebab house where we ordered some food.

'I'm having chips and garlic sauce; what are you having?' I asked Carys, even though with my gag reflex I wasn't sure I'd be able to eat them.

Some of the Asian men we were with seemed to know the guys behind the counter and soon we'd been invited upstairs. They were all Muslim so they didn't smoke or drink, but Carys and I knocked back the booze quickly as they began to come on to us. It was clear that we hadn't finished 'work'. Four men held me down and raped me before letting me go. Carys was equally shaken, so we got out of there and ran back to the flat where we found some other girls waiting.

'God, they look young!' I whispered to Carys, who nodded in agreement.

I was still only sixteen, but the ten or so girls there only looked about fifteen or younger. I wanted to ask their age, but we weren't allowed to speak to each other. Instead we just nodded and passed cigarettes between us. The group was already busy, chatting amongst themselves and, although I couldn't hear exactly what they were saying, I recognised the accent – they all sounded as though they came from Blackpool. I wondered if they'd lied to their parents as well?

An older, hard-faced woman unexpectedly appeared on the stairs. She was middle-aged, around fifty, and she stood there, staring directly at me and Carys.

'You two need to smarten yourselves up,' she remarked, taking us in from our feet to the top of our heads. 'Here,' she said, pulling out a purse and handing over a crisp £20 note, 'go and buy yourselves a dress each, and make sure it's a mini-dress.'

We didn't know why the old woman had given us £20, but we didn't argue either. I should have known better; no one gives you money for nothing.

The following day Carys and I woke early but in different rooms. I'd been split up from my friend, who had slept on the bathroom floor with a random guy. Meanwhile, I'd been told to sleep in a bed with some other men. They were still asleep, so I climbed over them, got dressed and went to look for Carys. Together, we tiptoed out of the flat and wandered into the town centre.

'Look!' Carys shrieked. She stopped dead in her tracks and pointed over at a shop window. 'Hair extensions! Oh my God! I've got to go in!'

Ten minutes later we emerged back onto the street, giggling and clutching a carrier bag. Carys had bought blonde hair extensions and some ridiculous long, false eyelashes.

'They're lush, aren't they?' she cooed as she inspected them in their packet.

I tried not to laugh – they were completely ridiculous.

'Yeah, if you say so.'

We wandered further along the same street and came to a stop outside a fancy dress shop. The window was full of crazy costumes including clowns, animals and pirates.

'Come on; let's go in for a look?' Carys suggested, grabbing my sleeve. 'That woman told us to buy a dress, and I bet they're dead cheap in here.'

I was just busy browsing in the shop when I heard peals of laughter coming from the back of the store.

'Em, Em, come here!'

It was Carys.

'Look!' she squealed, pointing up at something on a hanger on the wall. It was a black halter-neck dress that was cheap and tacky-looking.

'It's a hooker dress!' Carys sniggered.

Pinned to it was a large orange star with an 'Only £10!' price tag.

'Oh, fuck!' I gasped, bursting out laughing.

The man behind the counter looked up at the dress and then back at us.

'Want to try it on?'

Carys shook her head and pulled out the £20 note from her pocket.

'No, no, we'll just buy it. Can we take that one?' she asked, turning to wink at me.

Most people buy 'Kiss Me Quick' hats when they visit Blackpool, but not us. Armed with the hooker dress, hair extensions and false eyelashes, we found our way back to the flat. The property was next to a long row of sheds, so it was easy to find. The building had effectively been two flats that had been knocked into one, so the 'flat' – if you could call it that – was on two levels, with white and Asian men living on both.

The older woman was standing there, waiting for us on the stairs, as soon as we walked in.

'Well, how did you get on?'

Carys pulled the hooker dress from the bag and the woman placed her fag in her mouth so that she could inspect it closely. Her hands unravelled the scrap of material.

'Yeah,' she said, nodding. 'Not bad. How much was it?'

'Twenty,' Carys said as quick as a flash.

'And what are you going to wear it with? 'Cos you can't wear it with those,' she said, pointing at our trainers. 'No, you need to wear a dress like that with long boots and nothing else,' she said knowingly. 'Anyway, come and show me when you've put it on.'

Carys and I both tried on the dress, and she fixed the hair extensions in her hair. We wore it with long black boots and then swapped those for a pair of sparkly high heels.

'The boots look better,' the woman decided.

The fag was still in her hand. Ash fell from the end of it and sprinkled down along the stairs.

I wore the dress with a padded pink bra that I'd bought from the children's section at New Look. That's how skinny I'd become – I now had the body of a little girl. We tried our best to glue the eyelashes on but they were cheap and refused to stick, so we threw them on the bed. For the rest of the morning we hung around with half a dozen of the Asian men and then had sex with them. We never saw the woman again after that, but I wondered who she was. With hindsight, I suspect she was a madam, and the place had been a brothel. There had been a room downstairs that had long blue beads hanging from the doorway. We'd been told not to go inside so we hadn't. Although she'd given us £20 for the dress, I wondered just how much she and Yusuf had made out of us during that trip.

With our work done, Yusuf collected and drove us to another place – a huge house – in Wales, which was about ten miles from home. He'd arranged for us to 'meet' some more Asian men. I didn't know where we were but, with Yusuf gone, we had no way or money to get home. There were loads of men waiting for us inside the house – too many to count. Their eyes lit up as soon as Carys and I walked in through the door. We knew why we were there and so did what was expected. I lost count of how many men I had sex with that day, but I was bleeding so much that I had to try and stem the blood with tissues. We'd not been there very long when the men said they'd be nipping out.

'We won't be gone long,' one of the men said, speaking to us as though we were kids.

I glanced over at Carys because I thought it was such an odd thing to say. I'm still not sure what made me do it, but I sensed something wasn't right. I went downstairs and tried the door handle – it'd been locked from the outside.

'Fucking bastards! I don't believe it.'

'Whaa?' Carys said, running downstairs, wondering what on earth was going on.

'They've only gone and locked us in!'

She looked at me, then the door, and tried the handle herself, her face totally gobsmacked.

'The fuckers!'

The house had big windows but, try as we might, we couldn't prise them open to escape. There was nothing else we could do so we sat and waited. As the hours passed by, we grew more and more hungry.

'There must be something to eat in this bastard place,' Carys complained as she began to search through the kitchen cupboards. 'Aha! Here we go. Come here, you little beauties.'

Her hand dug deep towards the back of the cupboard and I craned my neck to try to see what she'd found.

'Ta dah!' she called out triumphantly, holding up two pot noodles. 'Now,' she said looking all around her, 'where's the bloody kettle?'

The hours dragged, so we smoked weed and waited for the men to return.

'Do you think they've gone to work, or something?' I wondered.

'I dunno, but they better bloody hurry back. I'm fucking freezing!'

I wrapped my arms around my own body to try and keep warm. Carys was right; the flat was freezing! We were still shivering when we hit on a plan.

'Let's have a bath!' Carys said, jumping up from the sofa.

However, it was an old system with a hot water tank, so we could only pour one decent-sized bath.

'We'll just have to share! Come on,' she said, lifting a foot to climb in. 'Ooh, it's lovely!'

'Hey!' I said, laughing as I stripped off my clothes.

The rest of the day dragged on but, eventually, around six or seven o'clock, we heard the rattle of a key in the lock followed by the sound of men's voices. They were back.

'Well, thank fuck for that!' Carys said, discarding a magazine she'd been reading onto the floor. 'Where have you been? We've been waiting all day. We've been cold and starving hungry!' she began, shouting at the group ringleader.

SMACK!

The noise reverberated across the room as he punched her hard in the face.

'Shut up, you whitey slag, and get up to the bedroom! You've got work to do,' he said, unbuckling his belt as the others laughed.

By now there were nine or ten men gathered, and Carys was forced to have sex with them all. I was forced to stay downstairs with another man, who had been told to sit and watch me. I heard noises, and felt guilty that I couldn't help. I wondered what I would do if I heard Carys scream. I pulled out my mobile but felt his eyes on me and the phone. I was worried he might take it off me, so I slid it back into my pocket and prayed it would be over soon. My eyes shifted over towards the door.

Run! Go on, do it! Run and get help! Do it! Do it now!

But I couldn't leave Carys up there alone. If I left, then God only knows what they might do to her.

What if they killed her?

I steeled myself as these and other thoughts flashed through my mind. Instead, I sat and waited; waited until I could go and see my friend. Finally, when the last man had come downstairs, I pushed past him to go to her.

'Are you okay?' I asked, bursting into the bedroom. I'd expected to find Carys in a crumpled heap on the bed, but instead she was sitting stark naked, smoking a fag.

'Hi, Em!' she said breezily.

'Are you … are you, okay?' I gasped, unable to believe just how chirpy she seemed.

'Yeah.'

Carys smiled and seemed nonplussed as she reached for her bra. She fastened it back on, sliding both straps onto each shoulder.

'But all those men … did you just have sex with them all?'

'Hmm hmm,' she mumbled, kneeling down to search underneath the bed for her knickers.

'And are you okay?'

She lifted her head and looked at me as though I'd lost the plot.

'Yes, Em, I had sex with them all – vaginal and anal, because some of them like that. What's wrong with you? Why are you shocked? That's what we came here to do. Now,' she said, stretching out a hand, 'pass me my jeans.'

Once the men had had sex with Carys, they seemed happy to unlock the door and let us leave.

'Mind how you go now, girls!' one said, laughing as he held the door open to let us out. I wanted to punch him in the face, but I held onto my temper. We needed to get out of there, quickly.

'Come on,' I said, grabbing my friend's arm, 'let's go.'

We were exhausted, thirsty and starving hungry, but we didn't have any money. My eyes darted all around, looking for something – anything – as we walked along a street full of terraced houses.

'Follow me,' I said, a plan beginning to form inside my head.

I tiptoed up to one of the doorsteps, bobbed down and scooped up a couple of pints of milk into my arms.

'Breakfast!' I said, shaking one of the bottles at Carys. She took it from me and we both guzzled it down greedily.

'Right, let's go home.'

Carys had already texted Yusuf, so we stood on a corner and waited for him to pick us up.

'You two get on okay?' he asked, as we bundled into the back of his car.

'Yeah, but we're starving,' Carys complained.

'Don't worry; we'll stop on the way back.'

But we didn't. Not that he cared how we felt, as long as we made enough money for him.

Afterwards, we visited Blackpool time and time again with Yusuf, but it was never for pleasure. We provided a service – sex. I didn't realise it then, but we were being trafficked and, just like Telford, we were taken to be used and abused – like lambs to the slaughter.

CHAPTER THIRTEEN

THE ARMY BARRACKS

I was still only sixteen years old when Andrea told me she'd got a summer job at an army barracks just a few miles inland from us.

'I could get you a job there, too, Em. I've got contacts,' she insisted.

Andrea explained some members of her family already worked there, so they'd put in a good word for her, and she'd landed a job as a cleaner.

'I could get you in, too, if you play your cards right. Go on,' she said, giving my arm a squeeze. 'Come and work with me; it'll be fun!'

'Okay,' I agreed. 'Why not? Put a word in for me, will you?'

Andrea smiled.

'Consider it done.'

So, a week or so later, when she texted me to tell me I'd got an interview I was thrilled.

Don't worry. U will b fine x she signed off her text.

But I was nervous because I didn't want to let her down or mess up. In the end, my interview – with a guy called

Paul – had been pretty straightforward. He asked me if I had any cleaning experience.

'No,' I admitted.

Paul shrugged.

'No worries, Andrea will show you the ropes.'

I beamed, relieved that I'd not blown my chance. After a few more questions, Paul asked what size clothes I wore.

'Why?' I asked suspiciously.

The hundreds of faceless men who had undressed and raped me over the years flashed through my mind.

'You need to wear a uniform; I need to know so that I can order you something in. I don't think we have anything that'll fit because you're skinny and Andrea had the last small uniform.'

I glanced down at my emaciated frame – I looked just like my friend. The gagging reflex I'd suffered hadn't gone away; if anything, it'd grown worse and reached the point where I found it impossible to keep most food down.

'Oh right. No problem.' I replied. I felt stupid for doubting him.

My uniform consisted of a boring light-blue polo shirt and black trousers. The job was pretty full-on, cleaning and polishing floors until they shone. But, of course, Andrea was delighted to have a partner in crime to work at her side.

'I told you that you'd get the job. We're going to have so much fun!' She squealed, her eyes glinting with excitement.

A few days later the army HR department issued me with a pass I was told I'd have to wear and show to get onto the barracks.

'It's great you've got this job, Em,' Mum said, wrapping an arm around my shoulders. 'I'm so proud of you.'

I was happy, too; this would be my first proper job, and I was determined to make it work.

The barracks was spread wide and covered lots of land. The wives of the soldiers lived in houses at the top of the camp, and training was held on the right, just as you came in through the gate. There was also a sergeants' mess, a NAAFI (canteen) and a Spar shop on site.

I'd hoped the money would be good, but I was flabbergasted when I heard I'd be getting paid £250 for four days' work – more money than I'd ever had in my life! I couldn't believe it. Having so much money meant I'd be able to buy my own things, my own cigarettes and booze. It also meant I wouldn't have to sleep with blokes to get it, not any more. This, I told myself, would be my new beginning.

On my first day, Andrea told me to follow her lead. She'd been working there a short time so I trusted that she knew exactly what to do.

'Right,' she said, showing me through to the room where we kept our uniforms in a locker.

'First, we need to get changed.'

Once we were dressed, I waited for her to tell me what to do next.

'Okay,' she said, lighting up a cigarette, 'now we have a fag!'

I was worried the boss might catch us.

'But aren't we supposed to be working?'

Andrea waved her hand to the side.

'Oh, there's plenty of time for that. Let's have a fag first. Here, do you want one?'

I reluctantly took one but I didn't enjoy it because I was worried I'd get the sack before I'd even started.

'See that cloth?' Andrea said, blowing the last of the smoke out through her nostrils. 'Pass it here and grab one yourself; we need to look busy, even if we're not.'

I followed her into the corridor and tried to look as though I knew what I was doing.

'That's right; look busy,' she encouraged me.

I wiped down the windowsills and did as she said. We'd been cleaning for a short time when Andrea broke the silence.

'So, do you like soldiers, then?'

I shrugged.

'I dunno, I've not really thought about it.'

I wiped down a windowsill with a cloth as Andrea grinned and carried on cleaning.

'Because I've slept with a few of them,' she added.

I put my cloth down and turned towards her.

'Really?'

'Yeah,' she grinned. 'And the Gurkhas? They're the best. They really know how to look after you.'

I wasn't sure what I was supposed to say so I just nodded. So that's what she'd meant by 'perks of the job'. I didn't think much more about it until the following evening. It was Friday, and we were walking along the street when Andrea stopped dead in her tracks and stared over at the shopping parade.

'There's some Gurkhas over there I know. I'm going to ask them to buy us some booze. You wanna come?'

I giggled.

'Yeah!'

As we approached, I spotted a bunch of soldiers standing together in a group outside.

'Hiya,' Andrea said, smiling as though she'd known them all her life.

'Andrea!'

The men cheered and she pushed them away playfully.

'Here, I don't suppose one of you guys would go in there and buy me and my friend some vodka, would you?'

The men looked at each other.

'No problem,' one replied.

'Oh, I'll give you some money,' she said, pretending to reach down into her pocket.

'No need. It's a present, from me.'

Andrea winked at him, and the soldier went inside the shop. Moments later he reappeared, clutching a bottle of vodka.

'Cheers!' she said, laughing, then unscrewing the top and taking a long swig.

'Here,' the soldier added, producing another bottle from behind his back. 'I got you two – one for your friend.'

Andrea squealed with excitement.

'I told you they were great, didn't I, Em?'

We'd just started to chat when two police officers appeared out of nowhere.

'How old are you?' one of the officers asked Andrea.

The squaddies seemed to melt away into the shadows.

'Twenty.'

'No you're not,' the policeman insisted.

'I am.'

'Right, go on; prove it then. You got any ID?'

She lifted her hand and patted down all her pockets. She was twenty, but she didn't have anything to prove it.

'I've forgotten it.'

At that moment his colleague stepped forward.

'Right, well, you won't be needing that, will you?' he decided, pouring the rest of the bottle down the street drain.

'It's mine!'

But the officer wouldn't listen.

'And that one. Thanks very much,' he said, taking the second bottle from her.

'It's my vodka. I paid for that with my own money. You can't just take it,' Andrea protested.

But the policeman wasn't interested.

'I can, and I will. I'll leave this full and unopened bottle down for you at the station. You can have it back when you come and claim it using your full ID. Understand?'

Andrea was furious because her boy-like skinny frame made her look much younger than she actually was and, without her ID, there was no way of proving her real age.

'Right, well. Have a good evening, girls,' the first officer said, smirking, before they both turned and walked off into the night.

'Bastards. The robbing bastards!'

It was Andrea.

Suddenly, we heard a voice from the darkness behind us.

'Want to come back to the camp? We have more vodka there.'

Her face lit up as she turned to me.

'What do you think?'

'Let's go!'

That night we returned to the barracks and went straight to the Gurkhas' quarters – which were inside an ordinary-looking house on camp. By the time we arrived there was another girl already waiting. She was older than us – about thirty. It transpired that she was married to one of the soldiers and, together, we all got smashed. Not long afterwards, Andrea and I went upstairs to have sex with a few of the men. It was the least we could do because they'd bought the alcohol. Usually, when men did that for me, I'd have to pay them in kind.

The following Monday we returned to work, only this time we had a plan; we smuggled in some booze in a couple of hip flasks that we'd hidden beneath our clothes.

'Ready to clean?' Andrea said, pissing herself laughing as she took another slug of vodka.

'Ready!' I replied, smirking while pretending to salute her.

That morning we cleaned and chatted long into the afternoon. Andrea confided that she'd already slept with a couple of the other Gurkhas.

'And some of the other squaddies. You should try it, Em – they really look after you.'

I shook my head.

'Erm, I'm not sure,' I said, rubbing a cloth against a stubborn stain on the floor. 'I just want to work and earn a bit of money.'

'But that's it, Em; this is easy money. Quick money. Anyway, it's up to you, but promise me you'll think about it?'

I nodded reluctantly, even though I wasn't interested.

The following evening we were told to stay on late because we'd be needed to serve drinks in the sergeants' mess.

'But I've never really done anything like that before!' I said, beginning to panic.

Andrea waved a hand away as though it was nothing.

'You'll be fine; plus, it's good money for a few hours' work.'

That night, after cleaning the barracks, I changed from my blue polo top into a crisp white shirt. I smoothed my hands along the fabric to try and iron out a few creases, and then I was ready – for my first shift as a waitress.

'If we're quick, we'll just have enough time to nip to the shop for some fags. Come on, Em, get a move on!'

I glanced at my reflection in the mirror proudly and thought how smart and professional I looked. For the first time in ages I actually felt good about myself. Sure, I was still a bit on the skinny side yet, here I was, with a proper job and regular money. Andrea had already set off so I ran to try and catch up with her. We bought a pack of cigarettes and walked over to the sergeants' mess.

'No, not in the front!' she said, tugging my arm as though I was a complete novice. 'We have to go in at the side, on the left. Follow me.'

The room itself was lovely, with starched tablecloths that covered every surface in a white, crisp blanket. There were big, fancy lights – not chandeliers, but something equally formal, hanging down from the ceiling and dimmed to create an atmosphere. There were half a dozen sergeants around each table with a wine and brandy glass for each one. The men looked super-smart in their navy uniforms which had a red ribbon running down one side. Almost all had been decorated with various medals. Others wore suits, but it was all men. There were no women, apart from those of us serving them. At one point I spotted a few armed soldiers wandering around but I wasn't sure if they were on duty to protect the mess or if they were there as part of the celebrations. We'd passed the armoury on the way and had seen soldiers sitting and cleaning guns. But, apart from that, there were no other weapons in sight.

The sergeants were drinking whisky, brandy and wine, and it was my job to keep their glasses topped up. I was so busy serving drinks that I hadn't noticed Andrea had completely disappeared.

'More whisky over here,' one of the sergeants called, clicking his fingers at me. I rushed over.

I glanced up momentarily to look for my friend, but she still seemed to be missing.

Where is she? I wondered, as I darted across the room from one group to the next. I didn't seem to stop. I filled glasses, fetched and carried, but there was still no sign of Andrea. I felt a tap on my shoulder and turned to find one of the soldiers standing behind me.

'Come with me,' he said. His voice sounded so serious that I thought I must be in trouble.

The sergeant walked over towards the entrance, so I followed. Then he went through it and strolled around the edge of the barracks with me close behind. I wanted to ask him where we were going, and what I'd done wrong. I even wondered if it might be something to do with Andrea.

Was she sick or injured?

Panic set in and my heart began to hammer.

'Er, where are we going?' I asked, finally plucking up the courage.

'Just follow me.'

I did as he said and followed him to a field where the army kept their tanks. The sergeant turned to me, and from the look on his face it dawned on me why he'd led me there. His hands felt rough against my skin as he pulled me to the ground, pinned me down, and ripped off my knickers and trousers. There was no conversation, just sex. I lay in the darkness – my back pressing against the damp grass and my face turned to the side – as he pounded my body. Numb and still in shock, I stared up at the dull, khaki-green paint of the heavy-duty tank parked at the side of us. A single tear drained down from my eye and came to rest against my cheek. I realised then that this had all been planned. There had been no real job, just this. I wasn't and never would be a waitress. I'd never hold down a respectable job because this was who I was and all I was worth.

I cursed.

Who the hell do you think you are? Why did you expect anything better? You were kidding yourself when you thought you were here to do some proper work. How could you be so stupid?

Once the sergeant had finished, he stood, pulled up his trousers and straightened his uniform. I watched as he smoothed his hands along his smart jacket, just as I'd done with my shirt earlier that evening. He adjusted his trousers so the front creases were just right, and then he left.

Flushed and embarrassed, I ran back to the mess. My eyes scanned the room, searching for my friend. Finally, after what had seemed like an age, I spotted her. She was standing over in the far corner of the room, smiling and giggling with one of the soldiers. I watched as she playfully tapped her hand against his chest and turned away. It was obvious she was in full flirt mode. I raised my own hand and waved her over. Moments later, she was by my side. Grabbing the sleeve of her white shirt, I pulled her into a far corner.

'Fuck, where have you been?' I hissed, my voice sounding harsher than I'd intended.

Andrea looked up defensively, a little annoyed with me.

'Sorry,' I said, beginning to backtrack. 'It's just I've been worried; I've been looking everywhere for you. It's just that …'

Words failed me as my brain scrambled, trying to search for the right ones. 'I've just had sex, outside, with one of the soldiers. He was a sergeant. He took me to the field, where they keep the tanks, he pinned me down and, well, you know.'

Andrea shrugged: 'Where do you think I've been, Em? I've been busy, like you.'

Then Andrea turned on her heels and sauntered off to serve drinks and God only knows what to these men, most of whom were married.

CHAPTER FOURTEEN

THE LIST

Andrea and I had been messing about in the corridor, trying as usual to look busy, when one of the squaddies overheard and popped his head out of the doorway of his room.

'Here, come in here,' he whispered, beckoning me over. 'You wanna come in?'

The squaddies' bedrooms led off the main corridor and were a bit like basic hotel rooms inside. We'd been working in the training quarters, where soldiers would come to stay as they trained. Most of the rooms held two men at a time, but the camp had been unusually quiet so lots of them just had one inside each.

I glanced back at Andrea, who was busy cleaning, or pretending to. She felt my eyes on her and looked up.

'Well, go on then!' she said, laughing as she pretended to shoo me away.

I felt a bit stupid, like a child, with her as my mother, telling me what to do.

The squaddie held the door open as I left her in the corridor and stepped inside. The room was pretty pokey, with not much space other than enough for a camp bed. The walls were crammed with photographs of what I presumed were his wife and children. They were all smiling; happy faces beamed out from each and every picture. I turned back to face him, but the soldier had already begun to strip off.

'Are you getting on the bed then, or what?'

I realised that I'd been set up again. Andrea had known full well why he'd called me into his room. My immediate reaction was to run, but where could I run to? She was standing outside and I knew she would just persuade me to go back in and get it 'over and done with'. The soldier was naked and waiting expectantly.

'Well?'

My body seemed to go into automatic pilot as I unbuttoned my trousers and let them fall into a puddle around my feet.

'Come on!' he said impatiently. He checked the time on his clock, resting on the bedside cabinet. 'I haven't got long.'

My body felt numb as I laid down on his bed – as cold and dead as a marble statue – as he proceeded to have sex with me.

Why had I expected this job to be different? How could I have been so naive?

Of course I was there to be used for sex – it had been the only thing I'd ever been good at.

How stupid that you thought you could ever be anything better.

Once it was over, I got to my feet, pulled up my knickers and trousers, and went to leave.

'Hang on,' he called as he lit a cigarette and pulled open the cabinet drawer.

'I haven't paid you.' I felt the blood drain from me.

Is that what I'd now become – a common prostitute?

My eyes flitted back over to the door. I thought of Andrea, standing on the other side of it. My heart rose and felt as though it'd lodged at the back of my throat. Then a fountain of bile whooshed up, lapping and scorching the back of my tongue.

'Here,' he said, placing some coins into the palm of my hand. I glanced down blankly, unable to make sense of them or the situation.

'Thanks,' I mumbled as I dashed over to the door, turned the handle, and closed it behind me.

Within seconds Andrea was at my side.

'Well, how much did you get?'

I felt emotionless and held open my palm to show her.

'Is that all?' she shrieked. She glanced over at the soldier's door in disgust. 'Cheap bastard!'

Andrea's fingers brushed against my skin as she plucked the pennies from my hand.

'Here, we can pool all our money together. I'm hoping for a few more this afternoon. You never know, we might make a bit of money!'

And that was the moment I realised why Andrea had been so keen for me to work at the barracks. I wasn't there to clean – I never had been. She'd wanted me to join in her business – having sex with squaddies for money. I wanted to shout and scream out, my voice echoing along the corridor so that everyone could hear.

I am not a prostitute!

But I didn't have the strength.

'What if I don't want to?'

Even though it had been barely a whisper, I knew she'd heard me. I felt her arm as it linked through mine.

'Don't be daft, of course you do. This is what we do, Em – girls like you and me. Besides, it's a laugh. These soldiers like us and, if they pay us a few quid along the way, what's the harm? Anyway, think of all the fags and booze we'll be able to buy!'

I unlinked my arm from hers and took a step back.

'Oh, don't be so fucking boring, Em! You must've known why I got you the job?'

I shook my head in disbelief – my worst fears had just come true.

'Anyway, I don't know why you're being so fucking prim and proper; it's not like you're a fucking virgin, is it?'

Andrea's words stung because I knew they were right. That's why I was there. It was all I was good for.

'Now,' she said, wrapping her arm around my shoulders in a chummy way. 'There are a few other soldiers I said you'd like to meet.'

The next squaddie was already waiting as I knocked. Just like the one before, his wall had been plastered with photographs of his wife or girlfriend. There was a happy picture of a little girl; she only looked about six, and she had a wide, toothy grin. I felt her eyes burn into me as I guiltily averted my gaze. This one, like the last, was also a father. At sixteen, I was technically a child myself. I wondered how he'd feel if, in another ten years, it was his little girl, standing here in a soldier's bedroom.

'Hurry up, I'm gagging for it!' he leered, licking his lips as he pulled me over towards him and pressed me down on the bed. His mouth moved towards mine as though he would kiss me.

'No, I don't kiss.'

He seemed offended.

'Okay, take it easy; there's a good girl.'

Strangely, even though I had sex with unknown men, I found kissing far too intimate – even more intimate than sex. Once again, I managed to remove myself from my body as he pawed, sucked, licked and bit me. I'd found a way to drift outside of myself and stay there as all these men forced themselves inside me; strangely, that didn't matter to me, but kissing did and was strictly out of bounds.

'Oh, Emily,' he moaned.

I was confused; we'd only just met yet he knew my name. The weight of his body crushed against my ribcage and I found it hard to breathe. Thankfully, it wasn't long before he'd finished. Finding myself released from the dead weight, I sat up and searched for my knickers, which he'd pulled off in a frenzy. My eyes were busy, scouring the room, when I spotted a single sheet of paper that he'd pinned to the wall at the head of his bed. In his rush to have sex with me, I'd not noticed it before. I'd missed the crude scribble of blue and black biro on a short list — a list of names. I read each one. Right at the very bottom I spotted three I recognised: Andrea, Beca and mine.

'What's that?' I asked, pointing at it.

The soldier twisted to see what I was looking at.

'The names?'

I nodded.

'Oh that's just a list of girls' names. You know, girls like you, who come here to have sex. I pinned it up on the wall so I know what to call the girl I'm shagging.'

He'd said it in such a matter-of-fact voice that I nodded as though it made complete sense, even when it meant anything but. It took me another moment to fully register my own name at the bottom.

'But how did you know what I was called? I didn't say anything when I walked in just now.'

The soldier began to snigger as though he'd been privy to a private joke.

'Your friend. She told me, didn't she? Most of the lads have a list; it's just I keep mine up there, where I can see it. There's nothing worse than calling a lass the wrong name while you're doing it, is there?'

My eyes felt dead as I looked between it and him.

'No, I suppose there isn't.'

'Here,' he said, stuffing a scrunched up fiver in my hand, 'take this for your trouble.'

I turned, opened the door and stepped outside. The corridor was empty so I picked up a cloth and pretended to clean. A few moments later another door opened and Andrea stepped outside to join me.

'Fuck! That last one just gave me a tenner!' she whooped excitedly, dashing over. 'Here, how much did you get?'

I uncurled my fingers to reveal the crumpled £5 note.

'Great! Only a few more to go and we'll have a fucking fortune!'

She grabbed hold of me and pulled me along to the next door and the next soldier. By the end of the day I'd lain on seven different beds and had sex with the same amount of men. The bedsprings pressed hard against my shoulders and lower back, and they left small indents in my skin. At the end of the day, when Andrea counted up our 'takings' she couldn't hide her excitement.

'We've made thirty quid between us. It's been a really good day!'

But it hadn't felt like a good day; it'd felt like more of the same, only this time my name had been shared, bandied about; I wasn't a person any more, I was soiled goods – something to be played with and passed around for the price of a cheap drink or packet of fags, depending on the soldier's generosity.

It was only my third day in the job when I glanced

through the window and spotted another young girl, who had dark hair, hanging around the barracks.

'Who's that?' I asked, pointing through the glass, as the girl crossed the yard.

'Her? Ignore her; she's the competition.'

Andrea sniffed and put her nose in the air as though the girl was a piece of crap.

'Competition?'

'Yeah, she kinda does what we do. You know her name is on the list, only she's a real prossie!'

My heart sank; isn't that what we were? Why did Andrea think we were any better than the girl? Were we prostitutes, were these men taking advantage of us, or was it a bit of both? Had it been sex or rape?

In my head, the boundaries had become so blurred that I didn't know what to think any more. Somewhere along the line I'd lost myself. My identity and self-worth had been taken from me piece by piece until I didn't know what to think or how to function. But I was there to do a job so I decided I might as well just get on with it.

By the end of that third day I'd had sex with countless soldiers – regular squaddies and Gurkhas – on rotation. Some of them didn't want sex but would pay to watch, with Andrea and I the stars of the show. By the afternoon we'd been invited back to one of the houses on camp to have sex with two older soldiers. One was Portuguese and in his thirties, while the other was a much older soldier whose nickname was Leo the Lion. Leo was in his fifties and I wondered what he was doing there. He was the oldest soldier I'd ever seen. After a bit of awkwardness on his part, the Portuguese soldier led me to his bedroom upstairs while Andrea stayed downstairs with Leo. I didn't speak Portuguese, and it was clear that he didn't speak a word of English and was extremely shy. With no conversation between us, I moved forward to place my hands on the top of his trousers but he pushed them away.

'Não!' he said in Portuguese.

I knew in an instant that he didn't want me to touch him. It felt strange, sitting there with nothing to do. I knew how to have sex with men – that was my comfort zone – but this was different, and I was unsure how to cope with rejection. Instead, we both sat in total silence, not knowing what to say or do. It felt like the longest five minutes of my life. Suddenly he stood and began to pace up and down the room. I was sitting on the edge of his bed but I felt so uncomfortable that I wandered back downstairs, and turned into the front room just as Andrea and Leo were removing all their clothes.

'Fuck off upstairs!' Leo barked.

I knew it was more of a warning than an instruction.

There weren't many other places in the house to go, so I went back upstairs to the Portuguese soldier's room. He seemed surprised when I came back in but, as we couldn't communicate, I didn't feel I had to explain myself. Instead, I perched myself on the edge of his bed and waited for Andrea to finish so that we could leave. I heard voices and the sound of footsteps on the stairs as the pair of them disappeared off into Leo's room for some privacy. There was a bit of a clatter followed by the sound of muffled voices. I glanced down at my hands and began to pick at a few loose bits of skin around my nails. But I felt too uncomfortable so I went to return downstairs. I was just passing Leo's bedroom door when I heard Andrea sobbing. I hesitated, unsure what to do. Leo was an imposing figure and there was something about him that really unnerved me.

'Andrea …' I called gently on the other side of the door. 'Are you okay?'

I pressed my ear against the wood, trying to listen for a reply, but all I could hear was her crying. Something was wrong.

'Andrea?' I knocked but there was no reply, only the sound of guttural sobs of someone in obvious distress.

Although I was scared of Leo, I put my fears to one side because I knew I had to do something. I had to help her. Turning the handle, I pushed the door open wide, but the sight that greeted me will never leave me. Andrea was kneeling on the floor, half-slumped on the bed, crying her eyes out. She was normally so confident and in charge that seeing her that way shook me.

'Fuck off, and shut the door!' It was Leo. His voice boomed over from the bed, where he was lying stark naked.

'No! I'm worried about my friend,' I insisted, nodding at Andrea, who looked pitiful on the floor. 'Come on,' I said gently. 'Come with me.'

She was still shaking as she stumbled to her feet. I could feel her hand trembling in mine as I led her towards the bathroom – the only space that felt safe at that moment. Andrea perched her slight frame on the edge of the bath and covered her face with both hands, as I went over to the door and locked it.

'Are you okay? What did he do to you?'

But she just shook her head and couldn't stop crying. I pulled at some toilet roll, wrapped it around my fingers, and handed her a wedge.

'Here, use this.'

She took it from me and dabbed both eyes. It took her a few moments, but eventually her cries subsided and she managed to steady her breathing.

'He just wouldn't leave me alone,' she began, her voice trembling with emotion. 'He was like an animal …' Andrea's voice faded to a whisper as I patted my pockets, searching for a spare cigarette.

'Here,' I said, handing it to her. 'Take your time. You're safe now; you're with me.'

But she couldn't stop shaking, even when she lit the cigarette. She took a long, considered lungful to try and calm her nerves.

'He's massive, too. I mean, he's really massive! I've never seen anything like it. I kept telling him to stop, that he was hurting me, but he wouldn't.' Her tiny childlike body trembled as she recounted the details.

'Andrea! Come back here now or I'll fucking …'

She physically flinched as Leo's gruff voice penetrated the wooden door.

'We can leave; leave right now,' I told her.

She shook her head. 'No. I swear, he'd kill us if we did that. And my clothes – they're in his room.'

I thought for a moment.

'You want me to come in there with you?'

Andrea's face lit up with relief.

'Would you? I mean, he might start on you?'

'Yes, but at least there'd be two of us. I'll protect you, and you protect me.'

My friend held out her hand and placed it on my knee.

'Thanks, Em. You're a real friend.'

Once she'd gathered herself and splashed her face with cold water, we walked back into Leo's bedroom, where he was waiting impatiently for us.

'About fucking time!' he complained, his eyes flitting between us both. 'Oh, but now I have two of you?'

I swallowed down fear that had risen at the back of my throat.

'That's right. Double trouble,' I said, forcing a smile.

But instead of having sex, I suggested we snort coke and smoke some weed first. I'd hoped that if we managed to get Leo completely off his face then we could escape. But Andrea must have been so exhausted from all the crying that she drifted off to sleep. I knew Leo might start on me, so I suggested sharing a B52 joint (a joint which contains cocaine and weed), hoping it would knock him out cold until morning.

'Come on, it'll be a laugh!'

I tried anything and everything I could think of to stop him from trying to have sex with me or my sleeping friend. Eventually, Leo fell asleep and so did I. I awoke with a start to find Leo lying on top of me, about to rape me.

'No!' I cried, trying to beat my fists against his face and body. But the more I struggled, the more he seemed to enjoy it. I tried everything, but I couldn't fight him off or rouse Andrea, who was still fast asleep next to us. With Leo pinning me down, I turned my face away as he brutally raped me. The pain was unbearable and I prayed it would soon be over. High on coke and weed, I fell asleep again, this time waking in the early hours. Thankfully, Leo was fast asleep and snoring like a giant, as I slid off the bed and tiptoed over to the other side to wake my friend.

'Andrea …' I said, shaking her gently by the shoulder. She shifted and mumbled something in her sleep. For a moment I was terrified she'd wake Leo. 'Andrea!' I whispered in her ear.

Her eyes blinked and then opened as she tried to focus on me.

'What the …' she began to mumble.

Leo momentarily stirred and my eyes were wide with horror; I lifted a finger to my lips as a signal for her to be quiet.

'Come on, get dressed. He's asleep. Let's go!'

Andrea fumbled in the darkness, her hands trying to locate her clothes, as we quietly padded out of his bedroom and downstairs. But the back door had been locked along with the front and there was no key in sight.

'Fuck!' I cursed as I searched all around. 'Window! We'll have to climb through the window.'

Andrea was high so she snorted with laughter as I pulled up a chair, opened the window and signalled for her to go first. She seemed a little unsteady on her feet, but I knew we had no other choice. The alternative was unthinkable.

'Come on, hurry up,' I said, pushing her back, trying to rush her.

'I'm going, I'm going …' she sniggered.

Thinking I'd heard a noise, my eyes automatically darted over towards the stairs. But no one was there. My senses were on full alert, listening out for Leo. I'd expected him to come thundering into the front room at any moment. But the groan and creak had been the central heating pipes, waking up for the morning. I turned back towards the window. By now Andrea had managed to climb outside and was shivering against the cold morning air. I hoisted myself up and pushed my body quickly through the window. My pink cardigan pulled as it snagged against something but I hadn't realised and tried to jump down onto the path. Instead of landing on both feet, I ended up dangling in mid-air. Andrea thought I was behind her and had already started to walk away.

'Help!' I called to her in a half-shout, half-whisper.

She turned to find me dangling – hung by my very own cardigan. I must have looked a bit of a sight because she promptly burst out laughing again. Soon she doubled over and couldn't help even if she'd have wanted.

'Stop it!' I said, joining in with her laughter while still high from all the chemicals snaking through my veins. 'I'm stuck. Help me! Help me, quick, before Leo comes downstairs!'

But Andrea was in hysterics and so was I; so much for my meticulously planned escape. In the end, the only way to free myself from the cardi was to pull both arms from the sleeves and leave it behind.

I'd felt guilty that I'd been chosen by the Portuguese soldier while Andrea had been lumbered with Leo. But I didn't feel guilty any more because he'd ended up raping us both.

'He raped me,' I said, blurting the words out to Andrea. 'When you were asleep. He forced himself on me and did it anyway. I tried to wake you, but I couldn't.'

Although she shook her head, she never said sorry.

'I wouldn't mind,' she said, trying to change the subject, 'but he's a fucking brigadier or something …'

I stopped in my tracks and looked at her.

'Is he?'

Andrea nodded and blew out a huge plume of smoke. My mind flashbacked to the weight of him, pushing and trapping me against the bed.

'I dunno, maybe not a brigadier, but he's higher than a

fucking sergeant, I know that for sure! Anyway, see that brigadier, who lives over there,' she said, pointing over to another house just visible in the far distance. 'He's as bad. He has young girls cleaning for him, he does. They're all at it, Em. They're all as bad as each other.'

I shook my head in disgust. So much for rank and respectability.

'Anyway, fuck 'em. Fuck 'em all,' she said, linking arms. 'Let's go to the pub tomorrow, after work. You wanna come? I know where we can get some free drinks.'

But now I knew – I knew without a doubt – there was no such thing as a free drink because everything had a price. Everything.

CHAPTER FIFTEEN

THE SOLDIERS' PUB

The scenery was breathtaking and I drank it all in as we sped along country lanes towards the pub. Andrea had persuaded three lads off our housing estate to give us a lift. We hadn't even considered how we would get home. I'd told my mum and Andrea had told hers that we would be staying at each other's houses. As we scooted along, one of the lads started to take the piss out of the driver, mocking him for not having a licence.

'What? You've not even passed your test?' I gasped.

The lad threw his head back and laughed.

'Nope. Why do you think I'm taking all the back roads?'

I glanced out and realised he was right. We'd not passed a soul since setting off. Instead, people had been replaced by a continual blur of green, rolling fields.

One of the other boys pulled out some cocaine and offered it around. We all took hits – even the driver. I told myself this was what life was all about when you're young – having fun. But looking back, my blood runs cold thinking of all the times I could've been killed, or worse – killed someone else in the name of 'fun'.

Soon we'd almost reached town. The driver indicated and pulled out to rejoin the main road running through it.

'Smarten up,' someone said as we finally reached civilisation.

We all knew it would be a disaster to be pulled over so close to our destination. We parked up in a car park and walked around the corner into the bar. It was a chocolate-box, picture-postcard type of place and there were tourists milling about in the street outside. The small Welsh town was a hotspot for them, just not that bar. It was strictly out of bounds to anyone but soldiers, and I soon found out why.

'Here it is!' Andrea announced as the lights from inside greeted us against the fading afternoon skyline.

The noise was deafening – a wall of men's voices all laughing, cheering and booming. It was utter bedlam. I immediately spotted long, white trails of cocaine lined up across the top of the wooden bar, as men of all ages cheered, laughed and slapped each other on the back, snorting up the powder through rolled-up banknotes.

'Yeahh!' the group jeered louder with the volume rising a notch, as Andrea and I – more fresh meat – stepped inside. The lads from our estate disappeared, trying to blend in.

There was no landlord, only squaddies standing behind the bar, serving themselves and everyone else to spirits and free ale. I watched as one – the glass already in his hand – walked along each optic, pushing a measure from each into it.

'Drink, drink, drink, drink!' his mates hollered.

They banged their fists hard against the bar, making all the empty glasses shudder and dance across it. The poor soldier looked down at the lethal cocktail he'd just been handed. Then he smiled and threw the dirty-coloured liquid to the back of his throat before balancing the empty glass upside down on top of his head. A loud cheer rose from the onlookers. Others whistled as the hapless soldier tried his best not to fall from the bar stool.

'Where's the landlord?' I asked Andrea, who was already making her way over towards the group.

'Oh, the squaddies just pay him and he leaves them to it. Doesn't give a fuck, as long as they give him enough money to cover what they drink. And they do. I keep telling you, Em, these squaddies are fucking loaded. They've nothing else to spend their money on.'

'Andrea!' a deep voice boomed across the top of the din.

I looked over to see Leo. He was sitting there, holding court with a group of other soldiers that I didn't recognise. I didn't have to look at her to feel Andrea flinch beside me. But she'd also felt obliged to go over and say hello to him, Leo slapped her hard on the backside as she reached him and the other men laughed in encouragement. I wanted to slap him across his smug face but, instead, turned and walked over to the bar. There were five other young girls standing by it but, one by one, they turned before disappearing off upstairs. A few moments later, Andrea wandered over to join me.

'Where are they going?' I asked her.

'There's rooms upstairs; they're taking the soldiers up there to have sex.'

'Oh,' I replied as a soldier handed me a cheeky Vimto.

We hadn't been standing there very long when one of the squaddies tapped me on the shoulder and asked if I wanted to go outside. I smiled and followed him. We passed some toilets on the way out, so he suggested we go in them to snort some coke. We did, and then he had sex with me. Afterwards, I pulled up my jeans and we went outside and stood in the pub doorway. He opened a packet of fags and offered me one. I was still smoking when he wrapped his arms around me, giving me a hug. I didn't care for him but I hugged him back and rested my hands on his bum. After I'd finished my cig, I crushed out the butt on the floor and wandered back inside to look for Andrea. My eyes were busy scanning the pub, when I felt someone behind me grab my arm tightly. I turned around to find the same soldier, standing there and glaring straight at me.

'Where is it, you little slag?' he hissed, spitting the words out in my face.

I was confused; I didn't have a clue what he was talking about.

'Where's what?'

'You know what,' he said, pushing up the sleeves of his shirt. It was clear that he was becoming more agitated by the minute.

'I don't; if I did, then I wouldn't be asking.'

The soldier rubbed the back of his hand aggressively across his nose.

'My fucking coke, you bitch! What have you done with it?'

I shrugged.

'Nothing; I haven't done anything with it. I haven't touched your fucking coke, all right?' I replied, turning away from him.

Before I knew what had happened I was sailing through the air, my feet stumbling against nothing as he threw me across the room. My body slammed up against the wall, and I fell so hard that I winded myself. I slumped down into a crumpled heap, my head resting against the skirting board. Everyone in the bar turned to look at me.

'Em!'

My name was being called by a familiar voice; I looked over to find Carys, battling her way through the crowd. 'Christ, are you okay?' she asked, helping me to my feet.

'Yeah …'

Carys turned and fixed the soldier with a filthy stare. 'Back off!' she shouted, putting her hand up to warn him off. 'Leave my friend alone, you fucker!'

But I'd had enough – enough of soldiers pushing me around and telling me what to do. I'd slept with almost thirty of the bastards over just four days, and had reached snapping point.

'Leave me alone!' I screamed at them all as they turned back to their drinks.

My friends had wanted to stay for more drinks, so I hung around even though I wanted to be anywhere but there. Later that evening, I was totally pissed and stoned when a man forced me to eat a whole chilli. Although he'd dressed it up as a joke, I knew exactly what it was – it was meant to control and degrade me further. I wanted to refuse, but there were too many of them, egging me on, and I knew I wouldn't get out of there until I'd eaten it. The chilli burned my tongue and the roof of my mouth, and it continued to burn long into the night – even alcohol couldn't touch it. To deaden the pain, I snorted even more coke and took MDMA.

Eventually, Andrea reappeared. I didn't need to ask where she'd been because it was obvious from her messed-up hair and dishevelled clothing. But by now I was so high that I was in a trance as one soldier passed me to the next. I was aware of them all; their fingers on my body, the sensation of multiple hands removing my clothes and of being passed between different men. But I was also too wasted to do anything about it – I couldn't stop them from raping me. It had been rape because I'd been far too gone on booze and coke to give consent. Once they'd finished with me, I stumbled on uncertain legs, and began searching the pub for Andrea.

'I … I … I need to go h … h … home …' I slurred when I finally found her.

The walls of the pub seemed to contract and bend sharply inwards. I put my hand up against one to try and keep both it and me still. But soon the whole room began to swim around me as though I was on a waltzer at a fairground. I felt so unsteady that I thought I'd throw up.

'They've gone,' Andrea said, piercing through the haze.

'G … g … gone? Who's gone?'

She placed her hand on my shoulder to try and steady me.

'The boys from the estate, so we'll have to wait. Wait until morning.'

At some point I must've passed out because, by the time I'd come to, it was already light outside.

'Come on,' I said, trying to rouse Andrea from a messy heap over in the corner.

The pub floor was full of bodies; there were soldiers laying all around, as though they'd landed where they'd fallen. It looked like a battle scene, only without a war. I searched behind the empty bar and spotted a taxi number pinned up on the pub noticeboard. I rang it, and a driver promised he'd be there within ten minutes.

'Andrea, come on,' I said, trying to wake her a second time. 'I've managed to get a cab. Let's get outside before anyone nicks it!'

The fresh morning air made me feel a little better but, try as I might, I struggled to piece together the events from the previous night. My body shuddered as I recalled all the countless hands on me, ripping off my knickers, pushing their tongues inside my throat and God knows where else …

'Is this him?' Andrea said, snapping me back into the moment.

The tyres of a long, blue battered car crunched against gravel as it pulled up and parked in front of the pub. The driver wound down his window and stretched across the passenger seat to speak to us.

'Taxi for Emily?'

'Yep!' I said, pulling open the back door. 'That's us.'

The cabbie seemed surprisingly chirpy for such an early time of the morning.

'Good night, girls?' he enquired, eyeing us through his rear-view mirror.

'Yeah, it was class, wasn't it, Em?'

I turned away and looked out of the window; I couldn't face anyone right now. Eventually, the cocaine and MDMA began to lift from my body. But the clock was ticking, and we only had a few hours before we were due back at work. With no time to spare, I got changed and headed straight over to the barracks. With the hangover from hell clamped tightly against my brain, I'd barely managed to function, when Phil called me into his office.

'You're lazy, and your work … well, it's not even your work because you don't even bother. Anyway, you can leave your lanyard and uniform in your locker because I want you gone. Don't even bother working the rest of your shift.'

I'd wanted to argue – to tell him I'd work harder – but I knew it would be pointless. In many ways I felt relieved, as though I'd been let out of prison, even if it had been a self-imposed one.

'Thank you,' I finally mumbled. And I meant it.

I didn't have the strength or desire to fight for my job because I didn't want to be there a moment longer. I was sick of being pawed, raped and passed around as a sexual plaything from one soldier to another. That morning I left, and I didn't look back.

Of course, Andrea had contacts there so she was able to keep her 'job', whatever that was.

'Why did they fire you?' Mum asked as soon as I explained why I'd returned home so early.

I went to open my mouth, to try and say something. I wanted to be able to tell her; to tell her what the men had done – how they'd pinned me down and raped me – but I couldn't.

How could I? Where would I even begin?

Instead, I just shrugged, and felt my heart plummet as Mum rolled her eyes in annoyance.

'I'm sorry.'

CHAPTER SIXTEEN
THE CHEMIST

There was a drug dealer who worked in a clothes shop close to our college, and her name was Alex. We first discovered Alex's drug sideline when we'd sat outside her shop one day in the sunshine, smoking weed.

'Like a smoke, do you?' she remarked, hovering in her shop doorway with her arms folded across her chest.

There was a gang of us smoking, and I was sitting with Andrea, my sister Lucy and our neighbour Ashley. I'd half-expected this woman to tell us to bugger off or threaten to call the police.

'Who wants to know?' Andrea replied, a little nonplussed.

'No, don't worry!' Alex said, holding up her hands defensively. 'I'm not going to tell, it's just that I can get you stuff, you know, whatever you need.'

'Like what?' I pressed her.

'Depends what you want?'

There was a moment of stalemate as we all sat there trying to suss her out.

'What about coke?'

Alex nodded.

'Speed?'

She nodded again.

'And weed, obviously,' she added, gesturing over at our half-smoked spliff. 'Like I say, anything you need, just come and see me.'

After that day, word soon spread and soon everyone at college knew Alex was the woman to go to if you needed drugs. With Barry off the scene, it had become increasingly difficult to buy drugs in the area. Fat Bryn was a bit too far to travel to by bus, which meant Alex picked up all our business because she was just so handy. Also, I knew if I bought drugs from a straight woman it would mean she wouldn't expect sexual favours in payment. In short, she provided drugs on our doorstep for no extra charge, and that suited us down to the ground.

Alex had a boyfriend called Fred, who I'd often see hanging around the back of the shop. He'd always be dressed in smart casuals and was behind the shop counter so often that it never occurred to me he might actually have another job. A few days later, I'd nipped into the toilets of a local pub to buy a pack of condoms from the machine, when I spotted a familiar-looking man sitting across the other side of the beer garden. It was Fred; he was enjoying a drink in the sun with Alex. Only this time he wasn't dressed in his usual casual clothes – he was wearing a uniform, a police officer's uniform.

I turned to Andrea.

'Look, it's Fred! He's only a fucking copper!'

I felt his eyes on me, and he looked straight at us as we hurried past. I tried to keep my face down, hoping he hadn't seen us, although I knew he definitely had. As soon as we'd bought the condoms we left by a different exit.

The next time we visited Alex's shop Fred was standing behind the counter as usual, waiting for her to lock up. I pulled out some money to pay for my phetamine and I expected him to say something, but he remained silent. Andrea smirked as though we were in on his dirty little secret, and he noticed.

Later that evening, I was as high as a kite as I stumbled in through the door at home. Mum was waiting for me; the weed I'd smoked had been so strong that it seeped out of my clothes and hair. She smelt it and demanded to know where I'd got it, but I refused to tell her. Undeterred, she began searching through my bag and my pockets, and that's when she found it – a lump of solid.

'Where did you get this?' she demanded to know.

I was so high and she looked so serious that I started to giggle. The more she asked, the more I laughed. She soon became exasperated and was just about to lose it when Lucy interrupted us.

'It was Alex – the one who runs the clothes shop – she sold it to her.'

My little sister hadn't meant to get me into trouble but she also didn't want Mum to completely lose it or be witness to a full-scale argument.

'Are you sure? The shop in town with all the hippy clothes in it?'

Lucy nodded, her eyes darting nervously between Mum and me.

'But how do you know?'

'Because I was there with Ashley when she offered to sell it to Em.'

I was so stoned that I couldn't begin to argue, so when Mum picked up the phone and dialled a number I didn't react. She was so enraged that she'd called a friend of hers – a police sergeant – who worked at the local station.

'There must be something you can do,' I heard her ask. 'She runs that shop in town. You know, the hippy one?'

Mum didn't know that Alex's boyfriend was a copper but his sergeant certainly did.

'Right, okay. I'll leave it with you, then. But if I ever find her selling drugs to my daughter then I'll take it further.'

The phone rattled as she slammed down the receiver and stormed off into the kitchen to speak to Dad.

I sneaked off up to my room and was lying on top of my bed when I heard the front door slam. Unbeknownst to me, she'd gone over the road to speak to Angela. Together, both women stormed over to the shop to confront Alex and tell her to stay away from their daughters. Mum hadn't realised it, but she'd just made the situation ten times worse.

A few weeks later, Andrea, Ashley and I returned to the local pub and I wandered over to the bar to order a Coca-Cola.

'Fat or skinny?' the barmaid asked.

I'd never heard the expression before and it made me laugh, which made a few people look over. With our drinks in our hands, we strolled outside into the beer garden; we'd just sat down when Fred appeared outside and looked over at me. My stomach knotted with anxiety but I pretended not to see him. A little later, I needed the loo, so I put my drink down on the table and went off inside to find the ladies. I had just unlocked the cubicle door when Fred came bursting in.

'Your mum wants to keep her big, fucking mouth shut!' he roared.

He was so close to me that I could smell the beer on his breath. Fred lifted both hands and shoved me so hard across the room that my stomach landed hard against the sink. 'You wanna fucking watch yourself!'

I was faced towards the mirror and I watched our reflections as he clamped both hands around my throat and began to grip so tight that I couldn't breathe. Then he spun me around so that I was facing him. I felt disoriented as he pushed me backwards into the baby-change cubicle – a separate room at the side of the ladies' toilets. Using all his strength, he slammed me up against the wall before using his other hand to lock the door.

SLAP!

The palm of his hand burned against my cheek before I'd even had the chance to see it; my skin felt on fire as he slapped me again and again until I fell against the baby-change unit. I could feel its hard plastic edge pressing against my spine.

'Tell her to keep her fucking mouth shut! Got it?'

SLAP!

I nodded as tears pricked at the back of my eyes. But I refused to cry; I wouldn't give the bastard the satisfaction.

'Understand?'

SLAP!

I nodded but by now he'd worked himself up into such a fury that he grabbed my neck again – holding me in a choke.

'I said, do you understand, you little slag?' Fred snarled. There was a sudden, sharp pain in my scalp as he wrapped his fingers in my long hair, and tugged my head to one side.

'Yes!' I finally gasped.

The word had lodged inside my throat as my scalp continued to scream; pain radiated from every single strand of hair as Fred tightened his grip.

'I could get into some real shit because of the drugs. And, if I get into some shit, then I'll take you down with me, understand?'

His vice-like grip tightened harder against my windpipe and I felt my face pulsate with blood. It collected above his fingers and throbbed inside my brain as he continued to choke me. Finally, he let go of my neck; I gasped for air and held both hands against it protectively. I was so distracted that I didn't notice his hand as it lunged against my jeans, ripping them open before he pinned me against the wall.

'I need to teach you a lesson,' he said ominously before yanking down my trousers and then my knickers.

Fred grabbed a length of my hair and wound it tightly around my throat, strangling me again. He unlocked the door and, with my trousers and underwear around both my knees, he dragged and then pushed me across the toilet into another cubicle. With my face pressed hard against the wall, Fred locked the door and began to rape me from behind.

His hands were still around my neck, applying pressure and crushing my face flat against the cold, plaster wall. I turned to one side just so I could breathe. My right eye smarted and then began to throb, and I could feel a bruise beginning to form on both it and my upper arms. A trickle of blood seeped down my face and its metallic taste flooded my mouth. The strong smell of disinfectant hung inside the cubicle as my nostrils flared, desperately trying to grab a lungful of air. Outside, people were laughing, joking, drinking, and the world continued as normal. Music blared from the bar and the sound of 'Round Round' by the Sugababes floated in from the pub, underneath the door. In a desperate attempt to remove myself from what was actually happening, I began to silently sing the lyrics inside my head, the chorus boomeranging around inside my brain.

I *needed* to sing just to block it out. To block out the grunts and groans, as Fred continued to pound at my body.

After he'd finished, Fred calmly zipped himself back up and left me there, bruised, battered and bloodied in a heap.

It'd felt like an age, but finally the toilet door creaked open and I heard Andrea's voice calling me.

'Em, Em! Where are you?'

'In here,' I replied, weeping.

'Christ!'

She pushed open the cubicle door and helped pull me to my feet.

'I saw him follow you but I didn't think he'd come inside the women's toilets!'

'He raped me! The fucker just raped me!'

Andrea was horrified as she glanced down at my jeans – the denim still pooled around my ankles.

'Em, you need to pull your jeans up.'

'I can't. I'm too sore!'

'Here,' Andrea said, dipping down to grab hold of my waistband, 'I'll help you.'

But it was as though a bolt of electricity had shot through my nether regions.

'No! It hurts; it hurts so much!' I screamed – the fabric cutting in against me.

'Try and do them up then.'

But I couldn't; my jeans were too tight because the belt had been built in to the waistband in a loop. It was impossible; they were way too uncomfortable and the crotch rubbed against the inside of my legs like sandpaper.

Andrea thought for a moment.

'Pull your top over them, then you can leave them undone.'

I did as she said, but I knew I couldn't stay there in case Fred was still in the pub.

'Can we go?' I begged.

My eyes darted nervously across every inch of the bar as I followed my friend outside.

'I think he's gone,' Andrea whispered, trying to reassure me. But I was frightened.

'We need to leave. Can we leave now?' I said, beginning to panic.

We sneaked out of a side entrance to avoid the beer garden, walked a short distance and sat inside a bus shelter. It had a perfect vantage point; I could see straight up and down the main road, so I knew I'd be safe.

'Wanna drag?' Andrea asked, lighting up a spliff.

But I didn't.

'What am I going to do?' I said, beginning to tremble.

I was so shaken by what had just happened – it had been almost as brutal as the prom rape.

'I think you need to speak to someone. Come on,' she said, pushing me into a nearby phone box.

Andrea picked up the phone and dialled a number. I felt the blood drain from my face.

'Who are you calling?'

'Childline,' she said, before turning her attention back to the phone. 'Hello, yes, I wonder if we could speak to someone. I'm with my friend and she's really upset …'

I shook my head; the last thing I wanted or needed was to speak to some do-gooder.

'Yes, she's safe. We both are, it's just …'

She looked over at me and mouthed 'What?'

'No!' I hissed.

'Oh, actually, it's more about me. I've been feeling so depressed recently …' she explained, suddenly changing tack.

I listened in disbelief as she went into a long explanation about herself, when I'd been the one who'd been raped. It was obvious the conversation wasn't going anywhere and, sure enough, after a few moments she hung up.

'Fucking useless!'

We stayed in the bus shelter for two hours until I felt ready to go back home. Mum called 'hello' as we walked in through the door, but I didn't answer. I couldn't speak to her. If she had kept her nose out of my business then none of this would have happened. Instead, Andrea and I went up to my bedroom where I slammed the door on Mum, Fred and the rest of the world.

The following morning, Andrea reminded me to go and get the morning after pill because I'd forgotten to take my regular ones. I knew the pill would protect me for up to three days. However, the nurse had become so pissed off by my regular visits that she made me swallow it in front of her. I suspect she thought that I must be getting them for other girls.

'It's not a form of contraception, you know?'

'I know,' I mumbled, my face flushing red.

But there was something else; all the rough sex had left me with something else – a problem that I couldn't keep running to my doctor with. All of us had suffered with them at one time or another, and soon urinary infections became the bane of our lives. Of course, we tried over-the-counter stuff, but they weren't always strong enough to shift the more severe ones. With no other choice, we turned to the local drug dealer – a guy called Daffyd the Chemist. The Chemist was a local junkie but, on our side of Wales, he was also known as an unofficial pharmacist, who could get his hands on any drugs, prescription or otherwise.

'I need something to get rid of the burning,' I confided in him one day.

'What are your symptoms?' he asked as though we were in the middle of a medical consultation.

I explained and then watched as he sorted through various bottles, checking the labels as he went. The Chemist discarded half a dozen before finding just what he was looking for.

'Now,' he said, fixing me with a serious stare, 'take two of these every day for a week and that should shift it. If they don't work, come back to me and I'll give you something stronger.'

'Thanks,' I said, before taking the brown prescription bottle with someone else's name from him.

'Now, do you need anything else? I've got some good weed, if you wanna try some?'

Daffyd held some out in his hand for me to check. I gave it a cursory sniff before he crumbled and then rolled some up into a joint.

'It smells like a fucking hedge!' I said, laughing.

He slowly inhaled the joint, blowing smoke out in a stream through both nostrils.

'It's good shit that! You don't know what you're missing.'

With Fred on my case and Alex presumably off the radar, I was desperate for weed, and Wales, it seemed, had run dry.

'Okay, give me some.'

Rolling my own, I lit and smoked it, and I planned how I could get my revenge on Fred. I decided Fred, Ivor, all police were the same, and I hated the fucking lot of them. In fact, I hated anyone in a position of authority.

'Fuck 'em all,' I said, taking a long, hard drag.

From now on I'd do whatever I wanted, and sod the consequences.

CHAPTER SEVENTEEN

HAIR AND FIRE

By the time I'd celebrated my seventeenth birthday I'd reached rock bottom. Soon I was getting into more trouble with the police, mainly for low-level anti-social behaviour. It'd become so bad that I started to be picked up on a regular basis, even when I'd done nothing wrong. My face had become known for all the wrong reasons, and it definitely didn't fit.

My spiralling depression affected me outwardly as well as on the inside. I decided that I no longer wanted to wear girly clothes because, in the past, they'd brought me nothing but trouble. Instead, I would hide my body, concealing my curves under baggy men's jumpers and loose-fitting trousers. From a distance, I looked like a boy; I tried to make myself look as unattractive as possible so that I wouldn't receive any unwanted attention from men. I'd had enough of that to last me a lifetime. I would scrape back my hair, scrub my face clean of make-up, and cover my body in dowdy and ugly clothes. I particularly hated my breasts and I'd swamp them in layers of clothing so that men wouldn't look at them or me. My mental health continued to deteriorate until I'd reached a point where I took some kind of perverse pleasure from feeling that way – lower than I'd ever felt in my entire life. I enjoyed feeling miserable and I wore my wretchedness as a comfort blanket – daily wrapping and smothering myself in sorrow.

Carys tried her best to snap me out of it; she gave me ecstasy pills believing they would help 'lift' my melancholy, but they didn't – nothing could, because only I could do that.

One day, in a bid to cheer me up, Bronwyn persuaded me to go out to a Young Farmers' Club event. They were regularly held in the countryside between Wales and Telford, and were usually inside marquees that had been erected in the middle of a field. There was always a bar and someone on hand to sell you drugs. The events were legendary and just an excuse for a big piss-up. I wasn't really in the mood, but with nothing better to do I went along anyway.

'Here, take these,' Carys said, handing me two ecstasy tablets before I left.

'Thanks.'

Carys looked at me and sighed.

'I just want to see the old Em again.'

'Okay, here goes!'

Throwing both pills to the back of my throat, I swallowed them down with a glug of water. Most people would only need one ecstasy tablet but I knew with my drug tolerance level that one wouldn't even touch the sides. Sadly, the ecstasy didn't lighten my mood in any way, shape or form. Instead it seemed to intensify the anger I'd been holding down deep inside – something kept buried. Just like with Pandora's box, I wasn't sure what might come flying out once I'd lifted the lid. So far I'd managed to keep it shut but, with my inhibitions stripped back like a raw nerve, I soon became a scrawling, screaming ball of fury.

Later that afternoon Brownyn and I arrived at the Young Farmers' Club. We were well on our way to getting really drunk when I spotted a familiar face through the crowd. There was a girl I knew, standing on the other side of the dance floor, chatting to her friends. The girl was called Alwen, who I'd known since school. We'd once been close, but had later fallen out over a couple of boys. We'd only been eleven years old when Alwen arranged for us to go down to a den; some boys had tried to put their hands down our knickers and Alwen had let them, but I'd refused.

It's all her fault! I thought irrationally. *That's where all my problems first started.*

Of course, it was totally a ridiculous thought, but in my drugged-up state it made perfect sense. Alwen was busy dancing with her friends when my anger ignited a fury inside. It felt like a steam train, coursing through my veins, until there was nothing I could do. Before I knew it I was up on my feet, marching across the dance floor until I was standing directly in front of her. Without saying a single word, I wrapped my fingers in Alwen's hair and pulled as hard as I could. She looked shocked and tried to step away from me, grabbing my wrist to try and free herself. But I didn't let go; instead, I pulled harder. A few farmers spotted us and bounded over to try and separate us, but my anger had given me the strength of ten men.

'Get off me!' Alwen screamed.

I refused to let go. The more they tried to part us, the harder I tugged, until a huge chunk of blonde hair snapped from her scalp and I wrapped it around my hand, like a golden ribbon. Time seemed to slow as I studied it woven between my fingers; her strands of hair shone beneath the disco lights, changing colour along with them and the thud of the music. Everyone stood there, staring at me in disbelief. At some point, Ashley and Beca pushed through the crowd that had circled us. Suddenly, Lucy appeared but no one dared say a word because the ecstasy had left me feral. Alwen and her mates were dressed up, but I was wearing jeans and a top, so I looked out of place. A scream pierced over the top of the music. It took me a moment to snap back into the present and realise the scream belonged to Alwen.

'She's pulled my fucking hair out!' she screeched, her voice slicing through the fog in my brain.

Alwen was clutching her scalp as her friends looked on, their mouths gaping open in horror. With the disco lights still flashing and the thud of the music booming in my ears, I held the small ponytail of hair up in my fist, like a trophy. In a drug-addled fury, I'd claimed my scalp for the night and I didn't care what happened next.

'She's fucking wild, that one!' I heard one of the farmers shout above the din.

A group of them grabbed hold of me and threw me outside into the blackened night. I sat alone on the grass, smoking joint after joint – Alwen's hair still twisted around my fingers. Beca came out to check on me, but I was rambling and didn't make much sense. Someone handed me a bottle of Smirnoff Ice, so I sipped at it and waited for the evening to end so I could go home.

Unsurprisingly, I was permanently barred from attending a Young Farmers' Club event ever again. Not that I cared. I didn't even like myself, so I had even less tolerance for anyone else. With Alwen's golden hair and the bottle still in my hand, I rejoined my friends. Someone offered us a lift home, so I climbed into the back of a car. Once we'd pulled up outside, I went straight to my bedroom. Mum and Dad were talking in the front room. They were watching something on TV, when Mun's voice called upstairs to me.

'Good night, Em.'

I couldn't be bothered to reply, so I slammed the bedroom door and glanced down at the strands entwined around my fingers. I curled and pushed them inside the bottle until Alwen's hair was coiled up behind glass, like a sleeping snake. Pulling open the bedroom curtains, I placed the bottle in the middle of my windowsill. I wanted to be able to see it – the 'scalp' I'd taken in anger.

So many men had taken a piece of me over the years, but now it was my turn. As the chemicals slowly began to disperse

223

and disappear from my body I knew it had been wrong, but I also felt an overwhelming sense of relief – relief that someone else was hurting instead of me. I'd become an animal. I had become so desensitised that I didn't care – about Alwen and her pain or about myself and the consequences of my actions. I didn't care about anything because I'd become paralysed from reality. Nothing could pierce my numbness, and I was terrified I'd never feel anything again.

Shortly afterwards, Ashley and I were out one evening, wandering around, bored out of our skulls, when I decided I needed to do something – anything – to try and 'feel' again. I knew I had to 'wake' myself from this numbness, so I decided we should burn something.

'Like what?' Ashley asked.

I glanced along the seafront, looking for something.

'That!' I finally decided, pointing towards an old wooden bus shelter. The shelter was empty and there wasn't a soul in sight.

'Come on,' I said, egging my friend on. 'Let's burn it!'

But Ashley was worried.

'I don't know, Em. What if someone sees us?'

'Just do it, for fuck's sake!'

Her eyes flitted over from mine to the bus shelter as she considered what I'd just said. Ashley picked up a few discarded chip wrappers off the floor and scrunched them up in her hand.

'Ready?' she asked, her eyes suddenly wide with excitement.

I nodded. Then I watched as she lit the paper and held it against a corner inside the shelter. After a moment the flames began to take hold. There was a sudden ignition and then they shot up, licking splintered wood that had grown worn and parched in the sun. I stepped back and gasped as a furious fire burst into life. Grinning maniacally, I stepped back as the flames climbed higher and higher. They charred both sides of the shelter before eating into the wooden slats of the roof. My eyes were wide and wild as I took in the glorious sight – the old bus shelter fully alight – yellow flames burning bright against the inky blue sky. I screamed and then I began to laugh. We'd done it! We'd destroyed it piece by piece!

I felt a tug against my arm and turned to see Ashley standing there. She looked absolutely horrified and stared at me as though she didn't know who I was any more.

'Fuck, Em! What the hell have we just done?' she gasped, her eyes fixed on the flaming bus shelter.

Without saying a word, she turned and began to run – away from me and the fire.

'Ashleeeyyyy!' my voice cried after her into the night. I watched as her darkened figure faded into the distance. 'Where are you going?'

'Out of here ... police ... fire engines ...' she replied – her answer fragmenting against the night-time sea breeze and crackle of fire.

I turned back to face what we'd done and felt the heat sear my skin. It scorched my cheeks and seemed to suck all the moisture from my eyes, nose and mouth. The flames were intense – real – but I still couldn't feel anything.

Why? Why couldn't I feel anything?

There was the faint noise of sirens – fire engines – as they sounded in the distance. I spotted the flash of blue lights as they approached, suddenly snapping me back to my senses.

I have to get out of here!

I began to run, tracing Ashley's footsteps into the night. By the time I'd caught up with her she could barely look at me.

'What the fuck, Em!' she said, still gasping and trying to catch her breath.

I slumped down at her side as we looked down towards the sea, the beach and the bus shelter – now a yellow ball of fire – against the sky.

Ashley had done it, but it might as well have been me because I'd all but struck the match. I didn't understand why I'd done it because I didn't have any answers, only an empty space in my chest where remorse should have been.

'Look!' I said, my eyes still manic as I focused on the unfolding scene below.

Two fire engines and three squad cars had arrived and I laughed as shadows below us moved quickly, trying to extinguish it before it had the chance to spread to a nearby bin.

In the days that followed, I wondered if life might finally catch up with me. However, it seemed I'd gotten away with it, like everything else. Everything in my life had remained hidden and concealed by lies, so I felt strangely relieved when two police officers knocked at our door. They had some questions they wanted to ask, including: where had I been on the night of the fire?

Of course, Mum was naturally horrified.

'You didn't have anything to do with it, did you?' she demanded to know after they'd left.

'No, I was nowhere near it. It's the police, they've got it in for me. I don't know why.'

Of course, I denied it all. I'd become adept at lying, but then a witness came forward, placing me near the scene. In the end I was bailed pending further enquiries yet, no matter how hard they tried, the police couldn't pin it on me. With the confidence of someone who thought they'd got away with it, my behaviour became even worse. I daubed offensive slogans on nearby buildings and hung around on the streets, picking arguments with passers-by. Eventually, I was charged with criminal damage for the graffiti and handed an anti-social behaviour order (ASBO). I'd been challenged to face up to my actions and take responsibility, but I didn't care. As part of my 'punishment' I was ordered to attend an anger-management course with the youth offending team, but I knew one course wouldn't make an ounce of difference.

'It's a fucking waste of time,' I complained to Andrea, as we sat in her bedroom, drinking bottle after bottle of blue WKD.

'Anyway, I don't give a fuck any more; I wish I wasn't here. I wouldn't give a shit if I died tomorrow.'

But my best friend didn't say a word; instead, she took a long and considered swig from her own bottle. She was sitting at the other end of her bed and seemed completely lost in thought. There was a brief silence before she looked up at me.

'Do you mean it?'

'What?'

'What you just said, about not wanting to be here any more?'

'Sure,' I replied, shrugging my shoulders. 'I don't give a fuck! Nothing matters, not any more.'

Andrea glanced out of the window. She scraped her thumbnail along the edge of the bottle, cleared her throat and then spoke.

'Let's do something about it then.'

I tipped my head back and drained the last dregs of my drink before letting the bottle fall from my hand onto the bedroom carpet below.

'Like what?'

'Well, if you don't want to be here any more, let's do something. Let's put an end to all this shit.'

I sat, waiting for her to elaborate.

'Like what? What do you mean?'

Andrea finished the rest of her drink and threw her bottle on the floor to join mine.

'Let's kill ourselves … and let's do it together! Come on, let's do it – me and you. Then all this shit will be over.'

I pulled myself up into a sitting position; she had my full attention.

'What? Like a suicide pact or something?'

She nodded. I felt my heart fly up inside my mouth with excitement and fear, and swallowed hard.

'But how? How would we do it?'

Andrea grinned and tapped the side of her nose with her finger.

'That bit's easy; just leave it to me.'

CHAPTER EIGHTEEN

PILLS AND LIES

In the weeks that followed, Andrea began to store up pills from home. She squirreled them away in her bedroom, hiding them in various pockets, bags, boxes – anywhere she could find. Her mum was a hypochondriac, so the bathroom cabinet was always full of medications for various ailments.

'Here,' she said, handing over a load of tin-foil blister packs. 'Look after these until I can get some more.'

'But how many more do we need?'

She shrugged. 'I dunno, but I think we'll need more than those if we're going to do it properly.'

I took the boxes of tablets, not even bothering to check what they were, and hid them on top of my wardrobe where no one would think to look. Soon I had a healthy collection – it was time.

I'm ready. R u ready to do this? I typed into my mobile phone, before sending the text to Andrea.

My phone vibrated with her reply.

Yes. I'll come to ur house later.

That evening I sat there waiting, but Andrea didn't show.

Where r u? I typed and pressed send.

Stuff happenin here. C u 2morra instead.

But tomorrow came and went and there was still no sign of her.

im doing it tmrrw. Will b in park at 7. See u there? I wrote.

My phone buzzed with her reply.

Yeh, c u then.

On my way to the park I bumped into Ashley, who tagged along, chatting to me. I had the pills tucked safely inside my jacket pocket, but I hadn't told her what I'd planned to do. Only Andrea knew.

'Are you okay?' Ashley asked as we walked along the street and down towards the park.

'Hmmm.'

She turned and looked at me oddly.

'Em, what's going on? It's just you've been really quiet lately, and you just don't … fuck it, I dunno, you're just not yourself. Have I done something to upset you?'

I shook my head and carried on walking, leaving Ashley standing there with her hands in her pockets. I carried on walking – my mind blank – because I didn't care about anything or anyone. I was just focused on killing myself and doing it properly.

Soon it'll all be over. Soon, you won't have to live this life any more. Soon …

'So, what is it then?' Ashley asked, interrupting my thoughts. She was a little breathless from running to try and catch me up.

'What's what?'

'You! What's wrong with you? And don't say nothing because I know something's not right.'

I stopped and turned, my feet scraping against the dirt gravel path as I did so.

'Trust me, you don't want to know, Ash.'

She shook her head.

'But I do; that's why I'm asking. Are you going to tell me what the fuck is going on, Em, or what?'

I gasped; exasperated that she wouldn't just go and leave me alone.

'If I tell you, then will you stop getting on at me?'

'Yes.' Ashley sighed in frustration.

Her breath rose up into a cloud of steam against the cold night air.

'Okay, I'll tell you then.'

My hand searched inside my jacket pocket and pulled out several blister packets of pills – roughly thirty or forty tablets. Ashley's eyes widened as she inspected them in my hands.

'Em, you're frightening me. What the fuck are you doing with all those?'

I ignored her question and wandered over to a grassy bit of the park. But Ashley followed and sat down next to me.

'Em, why have you got all those pills? What are you planning on doing?'

My eyes met with hers – I didn't care what she thought because my mind was already made up.

'Are you sure you want to know? I mean, really know?'

'Yes.'

I studied the multiple packets in my hands.

'Kill myself. I'm going to kill myself.'

Ashley gasped.

'Is this a joke, Em? Because if it is …' she said, clambering to her feet and backing away from me as though I'd just slapped her.

I shook my head.

'No; I mean it. I've had enough. I've had enough of everything, Ash. I just want it to be over.'

My friend was beside herself with panic.

'But what about your mum? And your dad? What about Lucy? What about … I don't know, everything?'

I shook my head as though all the fight had left me.

'I don't care,' I replied, my eyes brimming with tears. 'I can't do it, not any more. I've had enough. I'm so … I'm so … tired.'

However, instead of sympathy, Ashley became angry.

'Well, I'm not letting you do it!' she decided, trying to swipe the pills from my hand.

'No, Ash,' I told her. 'This is my life, and it's shit! You don't know the half of it; I've had enough and I just want it to stop – all of it. I just want it to be over.'

However, Ashley refused to give up.

'Well, I won't let you!'

I looked up at her in disbelief.

'And how the fuck do you plan to stop me?'

'I'll tell your mum,' she said, folding her arms across her chest defiantly. 'I'll tell her what you're planning to do.'

'I don't care. Do it! But you won't stop me, and neither will she because I'm going to do it.'

I turned towards Ashley, but she'd gone; her figure was already running away, to go and fetch help.

'Don't do it, Em!' I heard her voice call back. 'Wait for me! I'm coming back.'

But I was determined no one would change my mind. My hand searched my back pocket for my mobile; I needed to speak to the one person who cared – the only person who understood me – Andrea. I felt weak and emotional and I didn't have the strength to call her so, instead, I typed out a text.

Where r u? I'm in the park now.

I pressed send.

Seconds later, my phone pinged.

B there soon. x

But we supposed 2 do it together?

The phone vibrated in my hand as her reply came buzzing through.

U go first. B there soon. Don't worry, just take them x

I glanced down at the packets in my other hand.

Shall I do it now? I asked, pressing send.

Yes, do it. U'll b fine. Take em. But don't tell anyone u got them from me x

Pushing each pill out of its blister pack, they emerged – one by one – dropping into the palm of my hand. They

234

were all different sizes and colours, and I had no idea what they were or what they even did. That didn't matter – nothing mattered any more. Shaking them together into a multi-coloured heap, I threw them to the back of my throat and tried to wash them down with a slug of WKD. There were so many pills that I gagged and had to take a few more mouthfuls to clear them from the back of my tongue. Then I sat and waited. At first, I felt nothing and, for a moment, I wondered if they'd even worked.

Don't worry; they'll kick in soon and then it'll all be over.

I stumbled to my feet and wandered through the park a little further. Soon, each step I took felt even harder than the last. It was as though I was trying to wade through treacle. At seventeen years old, I felt as though life was already over.

What was the point in living? Life had only brought me misery.

I stumbled on until my legs became weak and unstable. There was a bridge on my left at the side of the park so I staggered down towards it. I laid down and pressed my face against the cool green, grassy bank and allowed it to chill my skin. Then I closed my eyes and waited for death to claim me.

CHAPTER NINETEEN

ANDREA

The lights above my head were so bright that they burned like acid against my eyes. My pupils had shrunk to small, black pin pricks and I blinked my eyelids in protest.

'Emily, can you hear me? You're in a hospital, you are safe and you're going to be okay. Do you understand?' a strange woman, hovering above my face, asked me.

I tried to speak but my throat felt as dry as chalk.

'It's fine,' she insisted, this time her voice a little more soothing. 'You lie back. You don't need to talk. Your mum is here; she's waiting outside. I'll go and fetch her.'

Moments later, Mum was by my side; her face looked suddenly old and it was creased with worry. Then I noticed her eyes were rimmed in redness as though she'd been crying.

'Hi, Em; it's me. How are you feeling?'

I turned my face away guiltily. Tears fell down from my face and soaked deep into my pillow. I couldn't look at her – it was too painful.

'The nurses and doctors, well, they've been great. They

236

pumped your stomach out, so you might be feeling a little bit sore right now.'

But I didn't react; I just stared at the wall.

'I looked everywhere for you, Em. Everywhere. Ashley came to find me, so I went out looking, and I found you there …' She stopped to try and compose herself, her voice trembling with emotion. 'I found you by the bridge. You were unconscious, so I called an ambulance.'

Mum took a deep breath and paused again as though trying to find the courage to continue. 'Anyway, I've spoken to the doctor and he thinks you're going to be fine. You don't have to worry about a thing. All you have to do is rest and try and get better.'

I felt the warmth of her hand as she clutched mine in hers.

It didn't work! my brain screamed. *You fucked it up! You can't even kill yourself properly!*

Mum didn't say anything else, not even when Dad came dashing in through the hospital corridors. No one said anything or asked me why I'd done it. It was as though everyone was treading on eggshells.

The doctors kept me in overnight for observation, and the following morning I was told I'd be discharged but only after I'd seen the hospital psychiatrist.

'Do you want to talk about why you did this, Emily?' he asked, resting back in his chair, as he studied me.

'Not really,' I told him.

I felt stupid, angry, even a little embarrassed, and folded my arms defensively across my chest.

The psychiatrist was still staring at me as we settled down into a long and uncomfortable silence.

'Did you wish to die?' he asked, making eye contact.

I shook my head. I just wanted to be out of there.

'No, it was an accident; I didn't really mean to do it,' I lied.

I hoped I'd managed to convince him so that I could leave his oppressive office and intrusive questions. He began to write a few things down and then told me I'd be referred for counselling.

'It's very important that you keep your appointments,' he insisted as he typed something into his computer.

'I will. I promise.'

But my eyes were already searching for the door.

Later that day I was discharged from hospital, with a handful of leaflets on things to look out for – jaundice of the skin or the whites of my eyes, abdominal pain, confusion or headaches. Thankfully, my overdose didn't have any lasting effects, only the feeling that I'd failed. In spite of this, a small part of me felt relieved, especially when I realised what I'd put Mum through. It was the worst part and it soon began to dawn on me just how selfish I'd been.

She doesn't deserve this. She doesn't deserve any of it; all she's ever tried to do was help me.

I knew she had so many burning questions she wanted to ask but didn't know how to. There was silence between us as we caught a bus into the centre of town. Mum treated me to a few DVDs, which had just come out and were still relatively expensive. But I still didn't feel ready to tell her or anyone else why I'd done what I had. Later that afternoon there was a knock at my bedroom door and she opened it holding a drink and a sandwich. I could tell she wanted answers. She needed to know why her seventeen-year-old daughter would want to kill herself.

'I didn't realise you were so unhappy, Em,' she began tentatively, skirting around the real question. 'If it's this place, then we can move.'

I was perched on the side of my bed and I glanced up at her. She looked so worried – her face so creased with concern – that it made me want to cry.

'I mean it, Em. We can sell this place and move away. We could get a fresh start somewhere else. What do you think?'

I looked down at my lap and shook my head.

'It's not that.'

She waited for me to elaborate.

'Well, if it isn't, then tell me what it is.'

But I couldn't. I couldn't tell anyone what was really going on inside my head.

How could I? How could I tell her what I'd been doing? How could I even begin to tell her about all the random men I'd slept with? Where would I even begin?

'It's nothing …' I mumbled.

Mum sighed and rubbed the heel of her hand against both eyes. She looked exhausted, as though she'd not slept for days.

'I'm just so tired of it all, Em. How can I help if you won't tell me what's wrong? How can me and your dad help you if you won't tell us?'

Her frustration was palpable and yet, no matter how much I wanted to share things with her, I knew that I couldn't. Instead, I sat there, mute and unresponsive.

Afterwards, I didn't bother to go to any of my counselling sessions – what was the point when I couldn't tell?

Unbeknownst to me, Mum refused to let it go. She'd bided her time and had searched through my mobile, looking for clues. My phone was an early, basic model, so it wasn't too difficult to navigate because it didn't have a pass code. She'd always made us leave our mobiles downstairs because my sister had run up a £300 phone bill by calling a premium number. But because she'd never looked before, I trusted Mum. However, my suicide attempt must have pushed her over the edge because she scrolled through my text messages until she stumbled upon some from Andrea. Mum was on the phone downstairs and I heard her say my name, so I ran downstairs. She was speaking to Andrea's mother, but by the time I'd reached the bottom step she'd already given her a piece of her mind.

'She encouraged my daughter to take those pills,' Mum insisted, her voice choking with emotion. 'What kind of friend does a thing like that? At her age, she should know better!'

I heard a raised voice answer on the other end of the line as it escaped the receiver.

'No, you listen to me!' Mum said, her voice raising a notch. 'This was Andrea's idea, and I've seen the texts to prove it. I've got it all here, on Emily's phone. It's here in black and white!'

There was another long, tinny reply. Mum was furious and pressed the phone close against her mouth so that she could shout down the line.

'Just keep your daughter away from mine! I don't want her anywhere near my Emily.'

She slammed the phone down in a temper and it rattled in its cradle.

'Unbelievable!' she huffed.

Mum glared over at me, her eyes still burning with rage. 'Andrea's blaming you! She told her mum it was all your idea.'

My mouth gaped open.

'Listen, I don't want you going anywhere near that girl again, you understand?'

'Yes,' I mumbled.

I was devastated that Andrea had blamed me, when it'd been her idea. I realised then I'd never be able to forgive her. Not ever. With our friendship effectively over, I began to hang around with a new group of girls, including one called Mari, who was friendly with my sister. Lucy had started going out with a boy called Gareth, who had a car, so he would drive us both over to Mari's flat. She was only seventeen, but she had her own place only a few miles away. Me and a few other girls would regularly go over to hang out there. Mari also worked at the army camp, and she would regularly bring soldiers back to her flat to have sex. Some of the others were shocked, but I didn't bat an eyelid because it'd effectively been my life over the past three years.

'You're so lucky,' I said to Mari one night, as Lucy and I sat waiting for Gareth to pick us up.

'Why?'

'Because you have all this,' I gestured around her flat with my hand.

'What? This shithole?' Mari scoffed.

I nodded and took a swig of WKD.

'Yeah, but it's yours, isn't it? You get to do whatever you like; you don't have your mum breathing down your neck like I do.'

'I suppose,' she replied, flicking open her lighter against another cigarette.

We sat for a moment and then she spoke.

'You could always come and live here, you know.'

I sat up on the sofa and rested my elbows on both knees.

'What? Here with you?'

Mari pulled the cigarette from her mouth and blew out some smoke.

'Hmm hmm.'

'Honestly? You'd let me move in with you?'

'Yeah, why not? You're round here all the time anyway. At least it'll save Gareth money on petrol,' she said, winking over at Lucy, who laughed.

I glanced over at my sister who'd been sitting there, listening to the whole conversation.

'What do you think?'

Lucy looked up at me – her face was excited but serious.

'I think Mum is going to go mental!'

CHAPTER TWENTY

SOULLESS SEX

'It'll not last long. You'll soon be back home,' Mum remarked, standing in the doorway of my bedroom and watching as I pushed the last few items of clothes into an overnight bag.

'Of course, you'll need your clothes washing. I don't suppose Mari has a washing machine, has she?'

I shrugged my shoulders because I couldn't remember. But the fact of the matter was, I didn't care. I needed my own space and, right now, Mari's flat would give me that.

'You will look after yourself, won't you?' Mum said, enveloping me in her arms.

I nodded.

'I'll be fine,' I promised, truly believing I would.

This would be a fresh start and, God knows, I needed that right now. Besides, I'd already put Mum and Dad through enough stress. Now it was time to stand on my own two feet, live my life and make my own decisions.

'Call me?' Mum insisted, pointing towards my mobile.

'I will.'

As I headed down the stairs and towards the front door, she called after me.

'You can come home any time you want, you know.'

'I know.'

In truth, although it had soon become my home, Mari's flat was a bit of a doss house for drifters and druggies. But, at eighteen, it had felt strange and exciting. I'd only been living there a day or so when Mari, who'd taken a soldier into her bedroom, came running out to find me. She was waving something in her hand.

'Look! Look what he's left me!' she squealed, as the soldier waved goodbye and left the flat.

In her hand was a crisp £10 note.

I'd been sitting, chatting to a few other girls on the sofa, but as soon as they saw the money they stood up and began to crowd around her.

'Do they usually leave you that much, Mari?' one girl asked.

Mari shrugged.

'Depends. Some do; I suppose it's how generous they feel.'

The girls looked at each other. We'd just sat back down when one of them came up with a business proposition.

'Listen; there are fifteen of us here, right?' she said, doing a quick head count.

I looked around the room. She was right; there were fifteen of us crammed into Mari's tiny flat.

'OK, so say each man we sleep with gives us a tenner, then that's £150. We could earn a fortune, as long as we keep the money to ourselves.'

I thought back to all the shady deals Yusuf had done; the blue, brown and red notes that had exchanged hands because of me and my friends. Mari had it right. No one was exploiting or making money out of her – she was making her own. Better than that, she didn't have to answer or take orders from anyone, and she could control who she slept with and when. Now that I'd moved in with her, I could do the same.

'I'm in,' I said suddenly as the others twisted around to look at me.

'And me,' another girl chipped in.

'Me, too!' replied another.

Soon, we'd all decided that this was what we'd do to get by – we'd charge men for sex. Although it was meant to be my fresh start, I didn't see what harm it could do. After all, I'd been giving it away free for years. Yusuf had thrown me scraps of money – the odd fiver here and there, and Barry had offered me the odd bit of weed, but I was eighteen now, and I was an adult. For the first time in my life I would be in charge of my own destiny.

We started up our 'business venture' later that day. It began with meeting some random guys in a town-centre pub and taking them back to the flat. After that we became a bit more organised, and Mari would bring soldiers back from the camp. Soon we had so much business that it was difficult to keep up with demand. The front room would always be full of writhing bodies, having sex in full view of each other and, just like the football club, Mari's flat soon resembled a scene from a Roman orgy. When we'd exhausted all the men in the area, we began to travel further afield to Cardiff, where we'd pick up men in nightclubs and scrounge free lifts home. One evening we were on our way back home when our friend's car broke down. Trapped at the side of the road, we managed to flag down a passing motorist and hitch a ride. By now it was the early hours of the morning, but the motorist – an old man – asked where we were heading. Even though it was miles out of his way, he offered to take us home, and we couldn't believe our luck. We were still high on drugs and booze when he suddenly pulled over at the side of the dual carriageway and demanded payment.

'But we haven't got any money,' one of the girls said, piping up from the back seat.

It was true; we'd spent the lot on drugs.

'Well, you're going to have to think of another way to settle your debt then, aren't you?' he leered, as he turned to face us from the driver's seat.

He was utterly revolting, but we knew we needed him if we wanted to get home.

'I'll do it. Go on, you lot get out,' the girl in the back seat bravely volunteered. She shoved the rest of us out of the car, and left us there, shivering at the side of the road.

My stomach turned as she proceeded to give him a

blow job, just to shut him up. We all waited for her to finish so that we could go home to our beds. But, stoned or not, the thought of her having to do that made me want to heave.

There seemed to be no shortage of men who were willing to pay for sex back at Mari's dingy flat. Business got so busy that we pushed the sofas together to form a makeshift bed so a girl could 'entertain' whichever man she'd picked up. More money meant more drugs, and our new business funded it. Sex meant nothing to me – it was absolutely meaningless, like a bodily function. All those years of being raped by different men had enabled me to disengage my mind from my body, just as I'd tried to do all those years before at the prom. To me, there was nothing loving about the act itself. During it, I would float above myself, as though it was actually happening to someone else. My body had become a vessel – a way of earning money – for drugs, and phetamine or weed were my ones of choice. As long as I could use them to blunt the soulless sex, I knew I'd be okay. My life had become a vicious circle and now I needed one thing to fund the other, and the second to blot out the former. The sad reality was I didn't like myself, so I didn't care what happened to me as long as I was able to get wasted. Unbelievably, I didn't even use protection – none of us did; instead, we'd go en masse down to the clinic at the side of the hospital for the morning after pill, knowing it would give us a few days' protection before we'd need to pay another visit.

There was a pub nearby, and the regulars in there knew us and the service we offered. One afternoon one of the punters – a man in his forties – asked if I'd give him a blow job.

'I'll give you £20.'

I nodded and told him to follow me back to Mari's flat. As soon as we'd walked inside I spotted her lying there, on the sofa, having sex with a man I'd never seen before.

'Won't be long!' she called, waving her hand.

Across the room there was a girl having sex with another stranger.

'It's okay,' I told Mari. 'He only wants a blow job.'

I knew it only required standing space, so I did it with him in the kitchen.

Afterwards, sex with strangers became so normalised that, half the time, someone would be cooking pasta in the kitchen while another would be earning money on the sofa. We could hear each other, but there were no rules and therefore no modesty or embarrassment. The men who paid for sex were mostly middle-aged, and almost all were married. Their visible wedding ring would give them away. The soldiers were obviously younger, and a little rougher, so we had to be careful to protect ourselves against possible violence. We did this with help from Emlyn, a bloke who lived in the flat upstairs. Emlyn was the local drug dealer, but he also became our protector. If any of the punters turned nasty or refused to pay, we'd grab a long broom handle and bang it against the ceiling.

Emlyn would be there in a shot, insisting on payment. In return, we each paid him £20 – around £100 a week – protection money, and he'd give us free drugs into the bargain.

I soon became really good friends with a girl called Ffion who was known by the nickname Cola.

'Why do they call you Cola?' I finally asked her one night.

'Because I like snorting cocaine.'

In truth, she was a really sweet girl, but she'd grown up in foster care and so had no family to speak of. I was immediately drawn to her because I'd felt like an outsider all my life, even though I'd come from a loving home.

Not long afterwards we were both sitting inside Mari's flat with Carys when we heard a fist thud loudly against the door.

'Police, open up!'

Carys had been busy straightening my hair, but my eyes looked in the mirror at Cola.

'What the fuck!' she gasped in a panic.

We weren't sure what to do, but I knew if we didn't open the door soon then they would batter it in.

'Coming!' I called out.

I signalled over to Carys to hide the stash of weed we'd just been smoking, and then opened up the door. There were two police officers standing there, asking for Mari. One of the neighbours had reported us for breaking into the flat because she'd seen us climb in through the window.

But we'd had to because Mari had left for work, taking the key with her. However, once the police had called Mari at work, the whole thing was cleared up and the officers left. But it had been a close shave.

If only they'd known what we'd really been up to.

Although I'd cut contact with Andrea, everyone had heard how she'd treated me. Mari was so enraged that one day, after bumping into her in the street, she'd walloped her so hard that Andrea decided to get even. Not only did she call the police and report Mari for assault, she also called at the flat and smashed the windows.

'She's fucking crazy!' Mari raged, peering furiously through the window to try and catch her red-handed.

Mari was still ranting and raving when Cola pulled me over to one side.

'Did Andrea get you to sleep with men for money?' she whispered, away from the others.

My mouth gaped open. I'd never told anyone about that.

'Yeah, why?'

'Because she did the exact same thing to me; she gave me to different men. I was just fifteen, but I thought it was normal.'

'Yeah, me too. I never saw it as anything bad because it just seemed that's what everyone else was doing.'

Cola nodded knowingly.

I thought back to the time I'd first broken contact with Andrea. I'd seen Cola and Andrea hanging around with one another. At one point Cola had been her shadow –

filling the empty space that I'd left behind. Once, I'd been walking along the street, minding my own business, when Cola came over and squared up to me, like a man would do. Without warning, she'd lunged at me; she was holding a knife and she'd tried to stab me.

'Know what you are?' she'd screamed in my face. 'You're a fucking slag!'

But now we'd become friends she felt nothing but shame as I recalled the incident.

'It was Andrea; she made me do it. Eventually I realised what she was like, and I knew I had to get away. That's when I started hanging around with Mari.'

Cola also told me how Andrea had tried to make her have sex with a boy she knew.

'In the end I did, even though I didn't want to.'

'And what about when you tried to stab me?' I said, bringing it back up.

'Yeah, it was all around the same time. I'm sorry, Em.'

I shook my head because she didn't need to apologise. She was a good kid, she'd just been desperate to keep her friend, as I once had. Up until that point I'd stuck up for Andrea. I thought she was my friend, and I'd followed her lead, right down to almost ending my life. I'd convinced myself she was the only person who truly understood me, but I'd been wrong. Then I thought back to the night at the prom and how she'd left me to fend off three men. I'd only been fourteen years old, and she knew what would happen – how could she not? Then there'd been the army barracks

– the dozens of men she'd help line up to sleep with me. My name had already been written down on the list before I'd even entered the room. Someone had given my name and there was only one person that could have been. The more I thought about all the awful situations I'd found myself caught up in, the more I realised there had been one common denominator – Andrea. She had been as bad as the men who had raped me over the years that followed. I'd been young and vulnerable, yet she'd identified my vulnerability and had exploited it to the full. She'd marked me out as an outsider – a loner – with no other friends to support me or watch my back. She'd taken me under her wing, just as she had Cola. Then she'd befriended and slowly groomed me to mould me into what she'd wanted me to become. It was only because of my suicide attempt and Mum finding all those texts that I'd finally managed to escape. Thanks to Mum, our so-called friendship had been shattered, but then Andrea had moved onto a new project – Cola.

'Don't worry,' I said, wrapping a reassuring arm around Cola's shoulder. 'I'll look after you now, I promise.'

And I did.

Mari's neighbours soon tired of men turning up at different times of day and night, and she was eventually evicted from her flat. As a result we all had to leave but, because she'd come from foster care, Cola had nowhere else to go. As she was desperate, alone and still only seventeen years old, I knew I couldn't leave her to fend for herself, so I took her back home to my parents' house. If I thought Mum would go mad when we both turned up on her doorstep, then I was wrong. Secretly I think she was relieved to finally have me back home. By then I'd lived or, more accurately, I'd survived at Mari's flat for almost a year. However, our lifestyle had been chaotic and dangerous, to say the least, and I'd been lucky to have lived to tell the tale. Although I returned with a new friend in tow, Mum welcomed me back with open arms. She knew at least if I was living under her roof then she'd be able to keep an eye on me. However, I found old habits hard to break and I abused Mum's trust. Cola and I would often bring men back to the house when everyone else was out. One of us would guard the door, while the other made a few quid for drugs. By now I was so hooked that I couldn't and didn't want to give them up.

There was a guy I knew who would pay us for phone sex. We'd talk dirty to him and he'd give us £20. But it was easy money and we didn't even have to leave the house to do it. By now, I viewed selling sex as my full-time occupation. The drug running, the grooming, the addiction to pills, weed and alcohol had set me up to believe that it was all I could do – sell my body to men.

It was around this time that Cola discovered she was pregnant.

'Christ, Em. What am I going to do?'

I wondered if she might have an abortion. But then she'd spent her whole life being shoved from pillar to post, so having a child of her own meant she'd finally have the family life she had so craved. Of course, Mum was brilliant and refused to turf Cola back out onto the street.

'She can stay with us as long as she needs to. I'll not see her out there on her own.'

I loved my parents, especially my mum, and I realised how she'd always been there, trying to protect me, even when I'd refused to listen.

Eventually, Cola gave birth to a little girl and I was there to hold her hand. Having a new-born baby felt, in many ways, like having a real-life doll. Up until that point I'd never had a single maternal bone in my body, but Cola's baby brought out a softness in me that I didn't even know I had. There was an alcove in one corner of my bedroom where we placed a laundry basket, padded out with sheets for the baby to sleep in. In many ways we were still kids ourselves – I was only nineteen and Cola just seventeen – so we treated her little girl like an accessory. Although we were far from responsible and still smoked weed, having a baby around gave us both stability in our lives. I still dabbled in drugs, but with a baby to go home to I stopped sleeping with strange men and started to look at life through a fresh pair of eyes. Mum and Dad would regularly offer to babysit so that Cola and I could go out for the evening. It was during one of those evenings that I first met Owain – a fateful encounter that would almost cost me my life.

CHAPTER TWENTY-ONE

CLOSE TO DEATH

'Come on,' I said grabbing Cola's arm one afternoon. 'Mum and Dad said they'd babysit. Let's go out.'

An hour or so later we were up at the school, waiting for a local drug dealer and friend called Owain.

'Look what I've got for you two!' he said, grinning while holding a clear plastic bag aloft as he approached.

I recognised the contents immediately – opiates (phetamine) and MDMA. I sat down on a nearby wall and rubbed phet into my gums as I'd seen the dealers do so many times before. By now I was an expert. Owain grinned as he pulled another small plastic bag out of his pocket.

'Wanna try something different?'

My eyes were wide as he opened the top of it to reveal some small, black poppy seeds. I was so smacked off my head that I didn't even care what it was.

'Sure! How do we take it?'

I'd never seen anything like it before in my life.

'We smoke it.'

Owain handed the seeds to me so I could look after them in case he got busted. Then he pulled out a Rizla paper and began to roll a joint, sprinkling the seeds into it. He lit the end and we passed it between us. As we did, the joint began to crackle and pop.

'What the fuck?' Cola said, pulling it from her mouth suspiciously.

'Oh, don't worry; it does that,' Owain said, laughing.

To this day I still don't have a clue what the seeds were, but I suspect it was opium. Soon it had started to rain, so Owain suggested we go back to his place to finish off our drug-taking. His house was a nondescript terrace that was situated at the end of a long row. It was absolutely tiny inside, but he showed us in and we all sat down in the front room. Then Owain stood up, turned on the fire, and placed the poppy seeds on the mantel above.

'When they dry you can use the liquid from them. It's much smoother,' he remarked.

With the fire on full blast, the tiny room soon became stifling hot.

'I'm roasting,' I complained, waving a hand to try and fan myself. 'Can we open a window or something?'

But Owain turned to look at me as though I'd lost the plot.

'And let all this heat out? No chance! Just take some clothes off – strip off a bit.'

He laid out some MDMA, and nipped out of the room. Cola and I weren't sure what to do, so we rubbed it against our gums. But nothing happened so we decided to try and snort it.

'Jesus!' I screamed, grabbing my nose and pinching it between my thumb and forefinger. It felt as though someone had lit a blowtorch inside both nostrils.

'Wait!' I called over to Cola. I put my hand up to try and stop her, but it was too late.

'Argghh!'

Her screams filled the room as she clutched at her nose and turned to me in horror. She was in agony – her eyes wild and streaming with tears.

'Aww, is it too strong for you?'

It was Owain; he'd come back into the room and looked at us both with disdain, as though we were complete amateurs. We probably were compared to him.

'Here,' he said, scooping it all back up, 'I'll make it into some tea so you can drink it.'

I didn't know if it was the effects of the drugs or the fire, but any inhibitions I might have had seemed to dissolve in the heat. Soon I was sitting in just my bra and knickers, completely zonked out.

'Here you go,' Owain said, smiling, as he reappeared with two mugs in his hands.

He handed us both a steaming cup of tea. The liquid was still too hot, so I blew across the top to try and cool it down a bit. In truth, it tasted strange and had a strong medicated tang and smell. It also tasted as though it had been flavoured with ear wax. I sipped cautiously. Owain also had some vodka, port and whisky in the house, so I took a swig of each to try to strip the strange taste from my tongue. Suddenly, and without warning, my heart began to hammer like a piston engine.

Thud, thud, thud …

It had started to beat so fast that I had to lean forward just to gasp for air. I clutched a hand against my chest to try and steady it, but it was no good.

'I think … I think …' I gasped, trying to take in more air to slow my manic heartbeat. 'I think I'm having a heart attack!'

I looked over to Cola for help, but she seemed out of it and was laid full length across the sofa. My body had no strength so I slumped down onto all fours. To try and support myself, I propped my top half over a small coffee table in the middle of the room.

'I need a pee,' Cola said suddenly. She stood up and headed over towards the stairs.

As I watched in my drug-addled state, I noticed the back of Owain as he followed her out of the room. They'd both left me. I'm not sure how long they'd been gone, but then I heard Owain's voice; it seemed to be drifting towards me from different parts of the room. My head felt heavy as I lifted it to try and locate where he was. I spotted him nervously pacing up and down the front room – he didn't seem as chilled as before.

'You'll be fine; deep breaths. Take long, deep breaths,' he said over and over again, as though he was some kind of doctor. 'That's it; breathe in, and out.'

I tried to do as he said, but my heart seemed to slow from a full sprint into a sudden crawl.

'Fuck! My heart … it's gone really slow!'

It was as though one minute I'd been running full pelt around a football pitch only to screech to a sudden and unexpected halt. My heart had gone from one extreme to another and now I was struggling to breathe. I placed a flat palm against my chest, but I could barely detect my own heartbeat. I was still on my hands and knees trying to breathe, when I looked up and realised that Cola was back in the room. She was laid across the sofa as though she'd never left it. Her eyes were closed and she seemed totally unresponsive as though she'd passed out or was dead.

I tried to sit, but couldn't lift myself up properly. Instead, I rested against the backs of my legs and began to claw at my bra strap. It felt too tight – a steel band clamped around my chest – and it was restricting my breathing.

'I can't … I can't …' I gasped, desperately trying to undo the clip at the back.

Owain slumped down in a chair opposite and began to grin. Finally, I pulled my bra off and took a huge gulp of air. I'm not sure if I'd taken in too much oxygen too quickly, but I became lightheaded.

'Air!' I gasped, trying to swallow down as much as I could in an attempt to kick-start my heart. 'I need more air …'

My body felt shaky and numb as I clambered to my feet and staggered towards the back door, pulling at the handle.

I was naked, apart from a pair of flimsy knickers, but I didn't care; I needed to breathe. The room was too hot and claustrophobic, and I knew if I stayed in it a moment longer my body would crumple beneath me.

'Need air ...' I gasped, half-standing, half-staggering.

The door handle twisted in my palm and the door swung open. I allowed the cool outside air to wash over me as I inhaled a greedy lungful. There was a large metal barrel that had been propped up against the outside wall, so I stumbled over towards it and slumped down. Owain followed me outside. I must have looked in a bad way because he knelt down and encouraged me to breathe.

'That's it; in ... and out ... in ... and out ...'

I did as he said, but I was still utterly terrified that my heart would stop.

'Don't let me die! Please don't let me die,' I begged him in between gasps and sobs.

Owain's hand rested on my knee.

'You're not going to die, Em, just breathe. Come on,' he said, clicking his fingers in front of my face. 'Stay with me. Breathe ... in ... and out ...'

My lungs snatched a mouthful of air as I took in a deep mouthful and blew it out through both nostrils. My eyes didn't leave Owain's, not even for a moment. I needed to focus if I wanted to live.

'That's it; in ... and out ... in ... and out ...'

I'm not sure how long I was outside, but even though it was freezing cold I couldn't feel a thing. My body, my skin, everything had felt numb. The only thing I could sense was the slow beat of my heart as I willed it to wake up and come back to life. The garden blurred in and out of focus as my heart kick-started, but my other senses seemed to shut down. Owain's voice came through in waves, as though he was calling to me from the end of a very long tunnel.

'That's it, just through here,' he coaxed.

Cold lino and then rough carpet brushed against the skin on the soles of my feet. Owain was there, at my side, propping me up as we walked back into the scorching hot front room. My arms and legs were peppered in goose bumps and I couldn't stop shaking.

Cola was still there, laid on the sofa. Even in my drugged-up state my eyes focused on her chest, and I felt a small spark of relief when I saw it rise and fall – she was still alive!

'That's it; not much further,' Owain's voice whispered against my ear.

There was a slight pressure – the feel of a hand against the small of my back – as I climbed the stairs. For each step forward, I would stumble back two. My eyes scanned both walls, looking for a banister, but there wasn't one. There was nothing to steady me, only Owain.

'Good girl, Em; keep going,' he encouraged.

Soon we'd reached the top of the stairs, and Owain stood behind to stop me from tumbling back down. We were on a narrow landing, but the doors, walls – everything – felt claustrophobic as though they'd all been built too close together.

'Want to go back to Colaaaa …' I slurred.

But Owain wouldn't let me.

'That's it,' he said, his voice filling my senses as the room seemed to warp and bend in and out of shape.

I felt a softness beneath my body and ran my hands over it.

Bed, my brain told me. *You are lying on top of a bed.*

I turned my face to see Owain standing in front of me, putting on a condom. I don't remember much else after that. When I finally awoke, I spotted a deflated condom lying on the floor at the side of the bed.

Sex. Owain has just had sex with you.

I felt disgusted.

You allowed that to happen.

But I hadn't. I hadn't even been conscious.

'Come on.'

It was Owain.

'You two have got to go. I've got my kids coming round this morning.'

There was a tug against my arm, so I sat up and tried to focus on getting dressed. I found my knickers at the bottom of the bed, so I pulled them on before going downstairs to search for the rest of my clothes. Cola was there, slumped across the sofa, but she also still seemed out of it. I shook her and hurried her along as we both got dressed and left the house without fuss.

'He had sex with me when you were on the floor,' Cola said, breaking the silence.

We were trying our best to concentrate on putting one foot in front of the other.

'I'd gone to the loo and he just followed me upstairs,' she told me.

I turned to face her.

'I think I overdosed last night.'

My friend stopped and looked at me in horror.

'I swear, Cola. I've never felt anything like it. One minute I couldn't breathe. The next my heart was going really fast and then it'd gone down to nothing.'

'Oh my God, Em …'

'I thought you were dead, too. You were on the sofa. Your eyes were closed and I wondered if you'd passed out … or died. Then I saw your chest moving, and I knew you were breathing. Christ, we could have both died back there!'

Cola stared at me with tired eyes; exhaustion etched across her face.

'But we didn't, did we? We're still here, aren't we? Come on, Em, let's get back. I'm absolutely knackered!'

'Yeah,' I said, grabbing her arm. 'Me too.'

It took ages to walk home; the after-effects of the drugs had left my legs weak and unsure.

It was early, and Mum and Dad were still in bed as we sneaked in through the back door and upstairs to my bedroom.

'I'm done in,' I gasped, allowing myself to fall back onto the bed.

'So am I,' Cola yawned, before collapsing next to me.

I fell into the deepest sleep I'd ever known. By the time I'd woken up I realised just how close to overdose I'd been. Luckily, I'd lived to tell the tale, but I knew there was no one else to blame, only myself. I'd chosen to take the drugs – all of them. I was still young, but last night's episode had proved that I wasn't invincible. No one was. Although I was living back at home, my lifestyle hadn't really changed. I was still doing it – living life on the edge. Something had to give, and it did. I didn't know it then, but I was about to meet someone who would not only slow me down, but would give my life a whole new perspective.

CHAPTER TWENTY-TWO

MEETING ROB

Carys sounded excited when she rang to tell me she'd landed herself a new job working for a building company.

'There are loads of men working there,' she said.

She didn't need to elaborate. New men meant money for sex, and more money meant we could buy more drugs. Although I'd found myself trying to move away from my old lifestyle, I couldn't give up the drugs – I was addicted.

Six months after that phone call, Carys and I had slept with lots of men. The sex had meant nothing – it was just another way to pay for what I craved – to function and stumble my way through life. I didn't have much time for men or boyfriends, for that matter. To me, there wasn't a difference. I had sex with different men and they paid me for it. I never kissed any of them, and I certainly never felt emotionally connected in any way, shape or form. That was until I met Rob.

It was the New Year, when Carys and I decided to go out drinking in the local bar. My eyes scanned the crowd, looking to see who was in, when they locked with those of a good-looking tall guy who was standing over at the bar. He looked different to all the other men. For a start, he had a large scar that ran from the top of his face to the bottom. It made him stand out, and not in a bad way. I'd just walked over to get myself a drink when he stepped over towards me.

'You want a drink?' he asked.

I tried to play it cool, even though I couldn't take my eyes away from his face.

'Yeah, vodka and lemonade, please.'

I turned to ask Carys what she wanted to drink but she'd already vanished into the crowd.

Instead, I studied the man as he waited to get served. His facial scar was extensive and it stretched from his chin right up to his forehead, tracing past, but missing, his right eye. Moments later he'd appeared with my drink.

'Thanks,' I said, stirring the cubes of ice with a straw. They chinked together as they swirled around inside the glass.

'Go on then,' he said, smirking.

I looked up at him, a little puzzled.

'Go on what?'

The stranger laughed.

'I'm Rob, by the way; what's your name?'

'Emily or Em, that's what my friends call me.'

'Go on then, Em,' he said again. 'Ask me how I got the scar. I know you're dying to.'

I looked down at my drink as colour flushed my face; he'd guessed correctly, I was dying to know.

'Okay, so what happened? How did you get that scar across your face?'

'A drug deal gone wrong. He stabbed me too,' he explained as he pointed to some shorter but deeper marks on the side of his neck. I felt him watching to see if it would put me off him, but it didn't. I was in no position to judge anyone.

'Right,' I mumbled, trying to sound unimpressed.

'But doesn't it worry you?'

I looked from my glass to him, our eyes meeting somewhere in the middle.

'No, not at all. In fact, what have you got to sell?'

Rob threw his head back and laughed because he realised he'd just met his match, and so had I. We chatted, drank and laughed long into the night. By closing time, when Rob asked me for my number, I scrawled it down for him on a piece of paper.

'Here,' he said, taking the pen from me, 'let me give you mine.'

After that we began to see each other regularly. From that moment on, I decided I'd finally found something I'd been searching for all my life – love. Now I'd met Rob I was a one-man woman, and from that day onwards I stopped letting other men use me for sex.

I was ten years younger than Rob, but I didn't care because I was completely smitten. For the first ever, I'd met someone who understood me completely. More than that, Rob didn't judge me – I'd finally found my equal. Sex between us was totally different to anything I'd ever experienced before. I was in love, and I craved Rob's scarred face and body. He was a big, strapping man, who didn't take any nonsense from anyone, so I knew he would protect me – protect me from all the shit I'd previously been through in my life. I knew he'd protect me from those who had used, abused and exploited me in the past. Just like me, Rob also loved drugs. He worked as a bricklayer and was staying in Wales on a temporary contract. He lived in a caravan near the building site. I don't know what I'd expected. but when he first took me back there I couldn't believe how clean it was.

'Christ! Do you have a cleaner or something?'

Rob's caravan was small – two berths – but it was tidy as a new pin, with not one thing out of place.

He saw my surprise and laughed.

'Nah, I'm just dead clean. I can't stand people being untidy.'

I gulped. My own bedroom was an absolute tip!

'Well, you better give me a bit of warning before you come back to mine. I'm a bit of a slob!'

But he didn't care because he loved me for who I was, and I felt the same too.

'I've met someone. He's great,' I told Mum a few weeks after we'd met.

She seemed relieved and happy that maybe, just maybe, I'd finally found some stability in my life. My face glowed every time I spoke about him. I couldn't help it. I found myself living inside a perfect bubble and I didn't want anything or anyone to burst it.

'Mum and Dad want to meet you; you wanna come around for dinner some time?'

Rob grinned but then his smile faded.

'I'd love to, but there's something I need to tell you first.'

My heart dive-bombed inside my chest.

Did he want to cool things between us? Was he moving away?

I scanned his eyes, trying to second guess whatever bombshell he was about to drop.

'I'm married.'

Air filled my lungs as I took a sharp intake of breath.

'You're married?'

Rob nodded.

'Yep, I need to be honest with you, Em. Trust me, if I wasn't, you're the one I'd be with.'

I felt my heart twist with pain as though someone had plunged a fist inside and wrapped it into a single knot. I thought for a moment and shook my head.

'It doesn't matter; I don't care. It's fine,' I told him.

In many ways it was. Although I'd fallen for him I knew that, by the very fact he was married, it meant this could never be anything more than a fling. A fling meant no commitment, and no commitment was a good thing, surely?

'And, your wife, where does she live?'

'Somerset. I go back there most weekends to see her.' Rob stared down at his boots, then raised his face to meet mine. 'That's not all, Em. I've got kids.'

I felt as though I'd been punched in the stomach.

'How many?'

'Four,' he said quietly. 'I love them, Em, I really do, but I never expected to meet anyone like you.'

I nodded sadly; I felt the same but I also appreciated his honesty.

'Well,' I said, a decision forming inside my head. 'What your wife doesn't know won't hurt her. As for your kids, I'd never do anything to destroy their lives, understand?'

Rob nodded. I knew it was a shit thing to do – to have an affair with someone else's husband – but I'd never felt like this about anyone before and I was determined to cling onto this small piece of happiness with both hands.

It's just a fling; just don't let yourself get in too deep.

A few weeks later, Rob was sitting at our kitchen table as Mum fussed around and laid dinner out on the table. I cringed as she and Dad asked Rob question after question.

'So, where are you from? How long will you be working in Wales? What is it you do?'

To his credit, Rob answered all her questions and more with good grace and humour, but I knew that he was blunt by nature, and it was only a matter of time before he told them the whole truth.

'I'm married,' he said, blurting the words out across the table.

Mum's mouth fell open; her eyes flitted from Dad to me and then back again. Her knife and fork were propped up in both hands as an uncomfortable silence fell.

'Em knows; I've already told her,' Rob added, nodding over at me.

I smiled at him and looked at my parents, who were still trying to digest the news.

'Well,' Mum said, getting up to her feet. 'I don't want your wife turning up at my front door trying to batter my daughter!'

I tried not to laugh; Mum was so protective of me. If only she knew what I'd already been through. I turned to Rob, grabbed his hand, and held it tightly in mine.

'It's fine. We're fine,' I insisted.

But later that evening Mum took me to one side.

'Be careful, Em. He's going to break your heart.'

I wrapped my arms around her and hugged her goodnight.

'What do you mean? I haven't got a heart!' I joked.

However, an uneasy feeling had nestled deep inside the pit of my stomach because I knew she was right. Before I'd met Rob I'd never shown any emotion – I'd been the ultimate ice queen. Then Rob appeared and somehow he'd pierced through my tough exterior and seeped into my heart. I'd fallen in love with him and there was no one – nothing anyone could say or do – to stop me.

CHAPTER TWENTY-THREE

THE PREGNANCY

I'd been living with Rob, spending almost every night with him in his caravan, for seven months when his building contract finally came to an end. Throughout that time he'd returned to see his wife and kids almost every weekend. But I was in love with him and I was willing to sacrifice anything, as long as he returned to me during the week.

'Where are you moving to next?' I asked, not wanting to hear the answer.

'The south coast.'

My stomach churned and I felt sick.

'But that's hundreds of miles away. What about us? What about me?' I said, emotion rising in my voice.

Rob held my hands in his and looked deep into my eyes.

'Come with me, Em. Leave Wales, and come and live with me down there.'

A small spark of hope ignited inside.

'But what about your wife and kids?'

'Well, I'll have to go back and see them, but I'll probably go every few weeks or once a month. It's a bloody long drive!'

I couldn't explain it, but his words caused my chest to crumple in on itself. So, it was a fresh start, but not really because I'd still be his fling – his piece on the side. But the thought of losing him for good didn't even bear thinking about.

'I'll come,' I said, cupping his face in my hands. 'I'll go anywhere with you.'

Mum wasn't very impressed when I told her, and neither was Dad, but they both knew how I felt and they also knew it was pointless trying to talk me out of it.

'Just be careful,' Mum warned, as I packed my bags and hauled them to Rob's car parked outside. The engine was running, and he was keen to hit the road to avoid the rush-hour traffic.

'I will.'

Dad hugged me, and so did Mum. Then she held me away from her at arms' length to take me in one last time.

'You ever need anything, you call me. Understand?'

'Yes. But don't worry; I'll be fine.'

That day, I left Wales for my new life down on the south coast. Naively, I'd hoped the distance between Rob and his wife would cement our relationship, but I was wrong. Before I left, some of his colleagues had warned me he had another girl on the go.

'A leopard never changes his spots,' one had said tellingly.

But I refused to listen. Instead, I shut myself off from the doubting voices and tried to stay there – right in the middle of my perfect bubble.

Rob and I carried on taking drugs, but we did it together. Instead of finding myself half-naked and half-wrecked in a strange flat, miles from home, I'd be safe inside the caravan with Rob. We were almost respectable in our domesticity. I'd wash up after dinner, he'd line up the cocaine, and then we'd snort it together. Often, he'd invite his mates around and we'd all get high. Even though I lived in the caravan, surrounded by his work colleagues, no one said or tried anything on with me because everyone knew that I was Rob's girlfriend. I wasn't interested anyway because Rob had become my everything.

We'd been living on the south coast for four months when I'd started to feel a little odd. He was heading back to Somerset that weekend to visit his wife and kids, so I asked him to drop me off at my mum's house in Wales.

Mum and I were sitting there in the kitchen, having a cup of tea and a natter when I blurted out something that had been weighing on my mind.

'I've missed a period.'

She sat back in her chair and studied me.

'Just the one?'

I looked down at the mug of tea in my hands.

'Yeah.'

'Does Rob know? Have you told him?'

I shook my head.

'No, you're the only person I've told.'

Later that afternoon she came home from town with something in her bag for me.

'What is it?'

'It's a pregnancy test; but you'll have to do it in the morning because it'll be more accurate.'

Later that evening my sister Lucy and her boyfriend Gareth invited me out for the night. Gareth lit up a spliff and automatically handed it over to me. But I looked at it as though he'd just given me poison.

'What's up, Em?' Lucy asked.

'I think I might be pregnant. I don't know for sure, but I don't think I should be smoking that.'

Lucy and Gareth began to laugh. It had seemed ridiculous to hear someone like me say something like that. In the end I decided to have a quick drag, but the smoke and the sensation of it creeping down inside my lungs made me feel nauseous.

'No,' I said, waving my hand away. 'You have it. I really don't want any more. Not until I find out.'

The following morning I was sitting on the edge of the bed with Mum, waiting for the blue tell-tale line to show me which way life would take me next.

'Well,' she said, removing the pregnancy test wand from my hands, 'you're definitely pregnant.'

I sat bolt upright on the bed.

'I'm going to get rid of it. I don't want a baby.'

But Mum wasn't convinced. My parents weren't religious, but they also didn't believe in abortion.

'Em, a baby is a baby. If you get rid of it then you are getting rid of a part of Rob.'

I knotted my hands together, my mind turning over the fact that I was going to become a mother when I didn't possess a single maternal bone in my body.

'But how could I look after a baby? I can barely look after myself,' I said, half-joking but meaning every word.

'Me and your dad would look after it. Anyway,' she said, rising to her feet, 'it's up to you. Speak to Rob, but don't make any sudden decisions. We are always here for you.'

With that she left. I thought about what she'd just said; how I could have the baby but that she would look after it.

That way, you wouldn't have to give up your life for a child.

I pulled out my mobile phone and dialled a number. Moments later, Rob answered. I knew he'd already be on his way back to Wales to pick me up but I needed to hear his reassuring voice.

'Hi, it's me,' I began, searching for the right words. 'Listen, I need to tell you something.'

Rob stayed quiet on the other end of the line and waited for me to continue.

'I'm pregnant, Rob. I've just done a test, and I'm pregnant. I'd missed a period, so I thought I better do one and …'

'Get rid of it,' he said, suddenly interrupting; his voice sounded stern and cold on the other end of the line. 'You'll have to get rid of it.'

I hung up and let the mobile fall from my hand onto the bed. I didn't know what to expect, but I'd expected so much more from him than that.

A few hours later his car pulled up outside my parents' house.

'Rob's here,' Mum called up from downstairs.

Normally I'd be excited – absolutely thrilled to see him – only not this time. Instead, I felt as though my heart had been ripped out and replaced with a lead weight.

'Hi,' I mumbled, as he took my bag from me and placed it inside the boot of the car.

Rob glared at me as though it was my fault.

'We need to get going,' were the only words he could muster.

Mum was still beaming as she waved goodbye and the car pulled away, heading for the motorway and the south coast. I didn't mention the baby and neither did he. In fact, we barely spoke a single word to each other all the way home.

Later that evening Rob's mates called around to see us. Someone cleared the table as another guy lined up three or four long hits of cocaine.

'It's pure, this, Rob. Just how you like it,' his mate said, before rolling up a tenner and snorting the white powder up inside his nostril.

He was followed by another man, and then Rob.

'Your turn, Em,' his friend told me, waving the rolled-up note so I could snort the last line.

'No. I'm not bothered.'

All three looked up at me in surprise.

'What? You? Not bothered?'

I shook my head. As I did, I caught Rob's eye. He was glaring at me as though I was the shit on his shoe.

'What's wrong, Em? You're not pregnant or something, are you?' one of the men said, laughing.

I shook my head even though he'd been bang on the money. I was pregnant, but Rob – the father of my child – couldn't even bear to look at me.

A few days passed by, but I didn't dare mention the baby or even try and broach the subject of my pregnancy. I was certain that, if I did, Rob would erupt. I sensed his anger – a bubbling pot of fury – building up inside him, and I knew it would only be a matter of time before he exploded. A few days later, Rob, his mate Sean and I walked down to the local pub.

'You want a game of pool?' Sean asked, nodding towards a pool table over in the corner.

Normally we'd all play pool together – the next person taking on the winner from the last game – but instead Rob sat down. Sean looked at me oddly as Rob sat there, nursing a pint in both hands. I picked up a pool cue, walked over to the table and grabbed the chalk. Sean seemed baffled but came over to join me; I continued to ignore Rob because I knew he was brooding and spoiling for a fight. I can't remember who even won the game, but at one point Sean and I started laughing about something. The legs of Rob's chair scraped loudly against the floor as he stood up and pointed over at us.

'I bet you've been having an affair with him, haven't

you?' he said, shaking with anger. He pointed at Sean, who was flabbergasted by Rob's sudden outburst. 'I bet you've been shagging him behind my back, haven't you? Have you two been having an affair? Is that it?'

Sean shook his head and so did I, but our denials only seemed to fuel his suspicion even more.

'I knew it!' he decided, thumping his fist loudly against the table. His bar stool fell backwards and slammed loudly against the pub floor as people turned to watch the unfolding scene.

'Rob, listen. You're wrong,' I said as I ran after him and tried my best to placate him.

'Fuck off,' he said, brushing me away. 'Just fuck off!'

Sean was still in shock when I ran back into the pub to grab my jacket.

'What's going on, Em? Is he okay?'

'He's fine, Sean. Sorry about that. Don't worry, I'll sort it. It's just an argument.'

However, by the time I'd reached the caravan Rob was still raging. If anything, he seemed even more wound up.

'I knew it. I fucking knew it! You've been shagging him, haven't you?' he said, slamming his clenched fist against anything and everything.

'No! I haven't. I wouldn't … I …'

Rob turned and grabbed me by the throat. Both his hands gripped the sides of my neck, his fingers denting my skin and crushing my windpipe. I tried to scream, but no sound came.

My eyes bulged in their sockets as he applied more pressure. Blood rushed and pumped loudly inside my ears as I struggled to breathe.

'Bitch!' he screamed, finally letting go. He shoved me hard across the caravan and my shoulder cracked against the wall as I fell against it.

'Rob, please!'

But he refused to listen. Instead, he grabbed me again, only this time I felt a white hot pain searing against the side of my face. He'd hit me; Rob had just hit me.

'Rob, don't,' I begged, cowering beneath him, but he pulled me up and threw me across the room again.

He continued to throw me around the caravan as I wrapped my arms protectively across my stomach to try and protect our baby. Eventually, Rob's anger began to disperse and cool and he slumped down onto the sofa. My fingers tentatively traced the skin of my neck, checking for damage. Without a word, I got to my feet, walked into the bedroom and began to pack my bag.

'Where do you think you're going?'

'Home, Rob. I'm going home.'

CHAPTER TWENTY-FOUR

WALES

It took him a few hours, but as soon as I saw the headlights flash across the darkened field I knew it was him.

'Hi, Dad.' I smiled as I opened up the passenger door. 'Thanks for coming to get me.'

My father looked both tired and worried.

'It's allright, Em. Just get in.'

I threw my bag into the back and climbed into the passenger seat, clipping the seatbelt around me. Dad leaned forwards to turn up the heating but, as he did, he noticed something and looked at me oddly.

'What have you done to your face?'

I automatically raised a hand to try and hide it; my skin felt hot and swollen beneath my fingers. Pulling down the passenger side mirror, I studied my reflection and tried not to react when I spotted my eye, purple and black from where Rob had hit me.

'Oh, that? I fell over. I tripped up on the grass a few days ago. Caught my bloody face against the side of the caravan, didn't I.'

'Hmmm,' Dad said, as though he didn't believe a word. He pushed the gear into first, let go of the handbrake, and then we set off, leaving Rob, the caravan and the south coast far behind.

Of course, Mum asked the exact same question as soon as I'd walked inside the door.

'She says she fell,' Dad said, answering for me as he shot Mum a knowing look.

'Right,' she replied tersely. 'You must be starving. Have you eaten?'

I didn't tell them it'd been Rob who had given me the black eye, but I didn't have to. But somehow I managed to keep the other fingermark bruises on my neck hidden from them and Lucy.

A few days later, Rob's name flashed across the screen of my mobile.

'What?' I answered coldly.

'Em, listen, I'm sorry. I've never done anything like that before. I'm so sorry. You're the last person I'd want to hurt. Come back. Come back home, and we can sort things out. I'm sorry, Em.'

I sat in silence. There was nothing I wanted to say.

'Em, are you still there.'

'Hmmm,' I mumbled.

'Em, I'm sorry. I miss you, please come home. I promise it will never happen again.'

Rob's voice crumbled and then he began to cry. I'd never heard him cry before and it startled me. 'I'm sorry, Em. I've never hit a woman before in my life. I swear. I just don't know what came over me.'

Somehow, his tears and apology cut through my anger and, against my better judgement, I decided to give things another go. I knew more than most that everyone deserves a second chance. I loved Rob and he loved me; we were going to have a baby, so I had to try to make it work, I just had to. He was the only love I'd ever had and I was determined to cling onto that. Of course, Mum and Dad weren't happy about it, but they knew I'd made my decision and, ultimately, it was up to me.

'You call us – it doesn't matter what time it is – just call if you need us. Anything.'

'Thanks,' I whispered, as Mum took me in her arms and we hugged goodbye.

Rob was waiting outside in the car, but she could barely look at him.

'Just look after her,' she warned.

I'd only been back at the caravan less than a week when Rob took something out – it was MDMA. I had a flashback to the night with Owain – the night I'd almost overdosed.

'What are you doing?' I asked.

'Oh, don't start; it's only a bit of this and Ket, Em. The lads are on their way over.'

Sure enough, moments later I heard a tap at the door. It opened to reveal two of Rob's mates standing there. Before I could say a word they'd both piled in.

'I hope you've not started without us,' one said, grinning, as they both plonked themselves down on the sofa.

Soon a whole array of drugs had been spread and arranged across the table.

Nothing's changed, and nothing ever will, a voice inside my head warned me. *You lived your whole life like this – you can't do it, not any more.*

I left the room, picked up my mobile phone and called my dad.

'Can you come and get me? I want to come home.'

I'd decided right there and then that I couldn't do it. I couldn't be pregnant, living in a caravan with drug-taking every other week. Although I'd never been maternal, a primal instinct kicked in and I realised I couldn't bring a child up in that environment.

My baby wouldn't stand a chance, I thought, as I pushed all the clothes I'd just unpacked back into the huge, black holdall.

'I'm leaving,' I told Rob after his mates had left, but he was so off his face that he couldn't or wouldn't put up a fight.

'How long are you going for this time?' he slurred, his eyes rolling back in his head.

'For ever. I'm sorry, but I can't do this. I just can't. Good-bye, Rob.'

I pushed past him, opened the caravan door and breathed in the cold night air. It was winter and the night felt absolutely bitter; a chilled wind whipped at my face and hair. Then I spotted the headlights of my father's car, and I walked towards them, him and a brand new start.

CHAPTER TWENTY-FIVE

LILY

Although Rob had begged me to come back, I knew that I couldn't. I had our child to think of now and, even though I'd never been the mothering sort I was determined not to expose a baby or any child to drugs. My whole life had been blighted by them; it'd started with Barry when I'd been eleven years old, and I knew I could never inflict that on another child. I was clean of drugs now, and had been since the day I'd discovered I was pregnant, and I was determined to stay that way. I owed my baby that, at the very least. Although I was excited by the prospect of motherhood, I also harboured lots of doubts as they gnawed inside my brain.

How will you cope with a baby, and are you ready to give up your life?

I wondered what I'd done and if I'd ruined my life. I also wondered if every new mother felt like me and had similar wobbles before the birth, whether they would admit it or not. Parenthood, by its very nature, is utterly daunting because there's no way of trying it out to see if you like it. Of course, Mum became more excited as my due date grew closer.

'Come on,' she said one afternoon, grabbing her coat off the peg, 'I'm taking you to Woolies. We need to buy that baby some clothes!'

Mum wasn't daft; she knew that once I'd started to shop for baby things it would make the whole thing seem real. We were standing in the shop looking at tiny outfits when I turned to speak to her.

'What if I can't cope? What if I don't want this baby? I've never wanted to be a mum. What if I can't do it?'

Mum gently laid her hand on top of mine and looked me straight in the eye.

'You can, and you will. And we'll be there to help you every step of the way.'

I knew she meant it. She'd already promised to bring my child up if I decided motherhood wasn't for me. It was a wise move because Mum knew that once I'd held my child in my arms, I'd find it hard, if not impossible, to walk away.

In January I was given a baby scan. Mum, Dad, my older step-sister, Liz, and Lucy all went with me. In fact, my family seemed more excited than I was. They sat and watched as the sonographer squirted some freezing cold clear gel onto my belly and began to scan the growing mound in my stomach. After a few moments she turned to speak to me.

'Do you want to know what you're having – a boy or girl?'

I looked over at my family – they all nodded excitedly. But I didn't need their permission – I was desperate to know myself.

'Yes, please.'

The sonographer pointed at the moving, grainy, grey image on the monitor as my eyes searched it, looking for clues.

'It's a girl!'

Everyone in the room smiled and cheered. Secretly, I was thrilled it was a girl because I'd already chosen her name. My baby daughter would be called Lily.

I'd remained in touch with Rob, who often popped in to see me to check on how I was doing. But I was alone with Mum when, three months later, I began to leak fluid. In a panic, Mum rang the doctor, who told her to take me straight to hospital. I was admitted and given steroid injections to try and strengthen my baby's lungs. Up until that moment I'd never been maternal, but right then I wanted nothing more than for my baby to live.

'What if I lose her?' I said, terrified. I gripped Mum's arm, my eyes wide with fear. 'I don't know what I'll do if she dies.'

Thankfully, Lily didn't die, and five days later I was transferred to Worcester hospital by blue-light ambulance because all the special care baby units in Wales were full. The journey only took an hour, but it felt like a lifetime as Lily threatened to push her way into the world.

Mum and Liz – a mother herself – were already there, waiting to meet me. Then Lily decided she wasn't ready after all and my contractions completely stopped. I was starving hungry, so Mum, Liz and I ordered curry, rice and chips in the hospital canteen. Even though I'd craved curry, it turned out to be a terrible decision because I brought it back up almost as soon as I'd eaten it. In the early hours of the next morning, around two o'clock, my labour pains started again. The onset was so quick and violent that I didn't have time for pain relief.

'Rob rang,' Mum said as she stood at my bedside later that day.

I grimaced as another bolt of pain seared through my body.

'Wh … wh … what did he say?'

'Not much. I told him you were in labour. I could hear him, but he couldn't talk because he was at some kind of barbecue with his wife.'

My heart plummeted because I knew Rob had chosen and, even though I was in labour with his child, he didn't care.

If he cared then he'd be there with you now.

But I didn't have time to think about Rob and how feckless he'd been because I was about to give birth and my baby needed me to be strong. Only a few hours later, Lily emerged into the world weighing 4lb 8oz, which the midwife said was a good weight for a premature baby. She had been born seven weeks early, and had to be fitted with a cannula in both her arm and foot. Healthy weight or not, Lily still had a battle to fight. She'd been born jaundiced and had to be placed under a special light and monitored by machines to help her breathe, feed and keep to the right body temperature. Day after day, I sat there, willing my baby daughter to pull through. It was during those early, dark days that I experienced a moment of pure clarity. Lily was mine; she depended on me, and I couldn't and wouldn't let her down. Even so, motherhood still absolutely terrified me and I would ask the nurse's permission just to pick up my own child.

'Can I?' I begged, unable to believe this beautiful little baby was actually mine.

Those early days in the hospital seemed never-ending but, day by day, Lily grew stronger until the time eventually arrived to bring her back home. My family threw us a huge welcome home party, which Rob unexpectedly turned up at.

'She's lovely, Em,' he said, lifting her from her Moses basket and cradling her tenderly in his arms.

I looked down at her; he was right, she was the most beautiful baby I'd ever seen.

'She's gorgeous … she's just so beautiful,' he continued to gush. 'I tell you what; I'll buy you a pram for her.'

But something kicked in. I didn't want Rob to buy Lily a pram; in fact, I didn't want him to buy her anything. He'd not been there throughout the pregnancy, nor had he attended her birth. He'd made his choice, and he'd chosen to go to a bloody barbecue with his other family.

'No, it's fine,' I said, taking her from his arms. 'You don't have to; I'll pay for it myself.'

'But, Em, I want to.'

I didn't care. Rob might be Lily's biological father, but that was it. I knew he couldn't be a real father to her because he already had a wife and kids waiting at home for him.

'It's fine, Rob. I'll provide for her.'

Although he continued to visit regularly, I knew our relationship was effectively coming to an end. Things reached a head when, six weeks after Lily had been born, he came to stay for the weekend. The three of us had gone out for a drive in the country when he parked up the car and turned off the engine. Then he shifted in his seat, placed a hand inside his jacket pocket, and pulled out two small bags.

'Look what I've got!' he said, waggling them between his fingers like a prize.

I knew immediately what they were.

'Coke? Rob, are you serious?'

He nodded and grinned.

'And these,' he said, waving another with blue pills inside. 'Viagra!' he said, starting to laugh.

But I was still sore and bleeding from Lily's birth, so drugs and sex were the last things I wanted or indeed needed. Rob's hand began to snake across my clothes but I slapped it away angrily.

'No, Rob. I'm still bleeding. I don't want to.'

But he was adamant.

'Come on, Em, you know you want to.'

This time I pushed him away. Suddenly, a vivid flashback washed over me – *all those men, all those hands, pawing my body*. My chest felt tight and my breathing became laboured.

'I said, no!'

'Okay,' Rob said, holding his hands up defensively. 'But what about some coke, you know, for old times' sake?'

I glanced back at Lily; she was sitting in her baby seat, slumbering soundly. My precious little girl, who depended on me.

'No! I told you. I don't do drugs any more.'

Rob sniffed and turned away.

'Well, you might not, but I still do.'

I twisted in my seat to face him, a bubble of anger rising up inside my throat as I wondered how he could choose drugs over his baby.

'Well, if you're taking coke then you're not staying with us. You're not coming back. I don't want that stuff anywhere near Lily.'

Rob tried to argue but I was adamant. That part of my life was over and I never wanted to go back. We drove back to my parents' house in silence. I climbed out of the car and unclipped Lily's car seat.

'Bye, Rob,' I said, knowing it would probably be the last time I'd ever see him.

That night he slept outside in his car because I'd refused to let him in the house. The following morning, by the time I'd woken up, Rob had gone and I felt nothing but relief. I looked over at Lily in her Moses basket. She shifted and stretched two tiny starfish hands up into the air as she stirred in her sleep; I knew then that I'd done the right thing. I crossed the room and stared down at her and felt an overwhelming wave of maternal love wash over me. This little girl had saved my life in more ways than one, and I was determined I would never let her down.

CHAPTER TWENTY-SIX

MOTHERHOOD AND MAKING A CHANGE

The following day Rob's name flashed up on my mobile.
'I'm sorry, Em,' he began.

But I'd heard it all before and I didn't believe it, not any more. His excuses had worn thin. I told him:

'It's not good enough, Rob. I don't want to see you any more, so you can just go. You're off the hook. I'll keep your secret until your other children are adults. I'll not destroy your family by going to the Child Support Agency – this is your fault, not theirs. I'll provide for Lily – we don't need anything from you and I'll never ask – so you have years to come clean and tell your wife you have another child. As soon as your youngest turns eighteen, that's when I'll go to the CSA.'

There was silence on the other end of the line as he digested everything I'd just said.

'So, that gives you ten years to tell her, Rob. Until then I don't expect a penny or anything from you. What you do now is your choice.'

There was another pause, and then he spoke.

'So, that's it, then?'

'Yeah, you're free to go – a free man. But once your youngest becomes an adult – when Lily is ten – I will ask for support.'

With nothing more to say, Rob hung up, and I never spoke to him again. Instead, when my daughter was two years old I got myself a job working in a baker's shop. Over the years that followed I worked long, hard hours and every penny I earned I spent on my daughter. I didn't believe in credit (and I still don't), so if I couldn't afford it I didn't buy it. In spite of this, my daughter never went without. Mum and Dad helped me enormously, just as they'd promised. When I first started working, I had planned to move out so that we could have a place of our own.

'What's the point in that?' Mum said. 'Live here for nothing – that way the money you'd pay in rent you can spend on Lily.'

'But don't you mind?'

She shook her head.

'No, not at all. I don't want to see you struggle. If you live with us then you can give her all the things she needs and more. Give her things you never had.'

In many ways, and with my parents' help, I managed to give Lily the idyllic childhood I'd craved. She joined ballet classes, played the guitar and piano, and she could swim from an early age. Lily is my child, and you will not find a prouder or more protective mum than me. In fact, because of what I've been through, I am overprotective of my daughter. I've only just started to allow her to play out in the garden with her friends ! It's because I'm aware of what can happen that I'm super-cautious. She's only recently got a mobile phone, but I know all her passwords for that and for social media, and I check them regularly to reassure myself that no strangers are talking to her.

I first began to suffer with severe post-traumatic stress disorder following my daughter's birth and, even though I've received counselling, it has never really left me. I haven't slept properly since the grooming began, and I constantly feel on edge, angry or out of my depth. Over the years I blamed myself for what happened; that I'd some-how brought it on myself. It is only now that I'm older and I have a daughter the same age I was when I crossed county lines that I realise it wasn't. I was just an innocent kid, yet I had my childhood stolen from me.

As Lily approached her eleventh birthday I knew I needed to do something positive, which is why I decided to write this book. It has been years in the making because I've carried these awful flashbacks and intrusive thoughts around with me like excess baggage. It took me a while to realise that I was a victim, but now I'm a survivor.

Today I pretend to give my daughter space, and I do, but I'm always there, watching and waiting for someone to try and exploit her. I'm also exceptionally harsh and uncom-promising when it comes to Lily's education because I didn't have one. I'm ashamed of my lack of qualifications, so I'm determined my daughter will follow a different and better path to me. I want her to do well so that she has the choices I never had. Education brings with it opportunities, and I want her to go out into the world and discover what it is she really wants to do. It's her life and, when she's an adult, I hope she will make her own decisions and mark on the world.

Lily often asks me about her father; I've told her he lives in Australia. Rob has chosen not to see her, but when she is old enough I'll tell her the truth. I'll also tell her what happened to me, although I'm frightened it might give her a negative view of the world and of her mum. But, in order to change things, we have to start with the truth.

I did keep Rob's secret for ten long years, but when his youngest child turned eighteen I contacted the CSA, just as I said I would. He's classed as self-employed, so he paid me for the first six months, and then he said his work dried up. That was two years ago, and I haven't received a penny off him since. However, he did call me to tell me that his wife had taken the news of Lily – his secret child – very badly.

'You had ten years to come clean,' I calmly reminded him.

As far as I know, Rob and his wife are still together.

Lily doesn't need her father because she is surrounded by the love of my family. My sister Lucy went on to have a child, and Lily is very close to all her cousins.

In order to come to terms with what happened to me, I began to raise awareness to prevent other children from going through what I had. In November 2018 I decided that in order to move on I needed to deal with the demons of my past. I approached the police to report historic child sexual exploitation (CSE) and slavery. However, police officers tried to dissuade me from taking it further. I still have correspondence, including texts on my phone, to back this up. Undeterred, a few months later, in January 2019, I contacted the Modern Slavery Helpline. I explained what I had been through from the ages of eleven to twenty years old, how countless men had raped and abused me. I'd been groomed from a young age and sexually exploited for over five years. I worked out that if I'd been raped by two men, three times a week, then this would equate to 312 men each year. Even by this conservative estimate it would mean that over that five-year period I had been raped 1,560 times. Sometimes the rapes would include eight or more men at a time, so it's difficult to calculate a precise number. But it doesn't matter because I still come to the same conclusion that over five years I'd been raped by over a thousand men.

The Modern Slavery Helpline explained that I'd been trafficked and had been the victim of child sexual exploitation (CSE). In turn, it sent an NRM (National Referral Mechanism – a process set up by the government to identify and support victims of trafficking in the UK) to the police. The only problem was my local police force didn't tell me it had received it. This only became apparent three months later, in April 2019, when I rang the Modern Slavery Helpline again. It told me my NRM had been sent over to the police in January. It felt like another in a long line of complaints from me about the police, which had messed up in more ways than one. It later transpired that long before I'd been gang raped on the promenade, Andrea – my so-called friend – had reported one of the men for rape. Andrea had been fifteen years old at the time of the offence but the police had wrongly recorded her as sixteen and so, as a result, it gave the man a police caution. Detectives explained the only witness to the alleged rape had been another man, who they insisted had since died. But he wasn't dead. In fact, the two of them were very much alive and had been two of the three men who had brutally raped me at the prom that night. The police had effectively allowed him and others to go on to abuse more children. I am now in contact with a solicitor to see if we can get some proper answers.

To this day I continue to suffer flashbacks caused by the abuse from my childhood. A short time ago I was picking Lily up from school when I spotted a police officer who had dealt with me as a teenager many years before. Without warning, I began to gasp and I struggled to breathe. My throat felt as though it had closed in on itself, and my heart pounded so fast that I thought I'd have a heart attack right there and then. Since that day I have to have someone with me every time I collect Lily from school. As a result, I referred myself for counselling. I needed to get rid of the demons inside my head that had plagued my every waking and sleeping hour; I needed to be rid of the anxiety, panic attacks and constant flashbacks; above all, I needed to sleep.

In January 2019 I met with Kirsty Williams, the Minister for Education for Wales, to tell her my story to try and raise awareness and get help from those in power. Initially I found her very supportive. She'd listened to my story and contacted the police on my behalf; however, then everything seemed to go quiet. I wondered if it was because of my experience of 'education' at the college that had led to me (and other girls) being groomed for CSE?

Around this time I worked alongside official researchers to try and change the way police deal with survivors of modern slavery and CSE. But my main source of help was from the Human Trafficking Foundation (HTF), which has been invaluable as part of my recovery, along with the charity SPACE (Stop & Prevent Adolescent Criminal Exploitation). Both organisations have been absolutely brilliant (please see the back of this book for more information and their contact details).

Last year, the Home Office NRM referred me to the Salvation Army (which is the non-governmental organisation – NGO – the Home Office sub-contracts to provide support and assistance to victims of trafficking in NRM cases), which I was told would offer me face-to-face support. It referred me to BAWSO – an organisation that specialises in providing information, advice and support to victims of abuse amongst the ethnic minority communities in Wales. I'm not racist, but I'd requested a white support worker because I'd been raped mainly by Asian men. However, the Salvation Army informed me there was no white support worker available. Refusing to give up, I went back to the HTF, which managed to secure me help from Black Country Women's Aid in Birmingham, which has been a lifesaver. If it hadn't been for the HTF, I think I would have given up. The brilliant SPACE also helped me come to terms with what happened to me from the age of eleven, when I was used as a drug runner. Receiving support doesn't change my past, but it helps me to come to terms with it and realise that none of it was my fault.

Even with my NRM, because I'm in Wales, the only support I have is over the phone. My solicitor has told me this is inadequate and that I should be receiving support to meet my trafficking needs and help me to recover, which includes face-to-face support. My only support is from someone I have never met, based two hundred miles away. Worryingly, I could actually be at home being re-trafficked with cuts, bruises and a black eye, and no one would ever know. At the time of writing this I've been in the NRM for eleven months. I'm supposed to have waited forty-five days, but my wait has been much longer. However, some victims have waited months, even years, and the Home Office is culpable. I believe it has failed me and so many others. I also feel let down by the support provided to me under the NRM.

I managed to secure counselling myself through my own GP but, even then, I have only been entitled to a dozen sessions, which hasn't been enough to deal with my deep-rooted anxiety and PTSD.

More recently I've spoken to the Children's Commissioner for Wales. I've also been asked to give evidence to a proposed independent inquiry into CSE in Telford. The inquiry, which was commissioned by Telford and Wrekin Council in April 2018, was set up after the *Sunday Mirror* newspaper claimed around a thousand girls had been abused by gangs operating in Telford since the 1980s.

I'm also on Twitter, where I try to help and advise other young women, like me, who have been victims of grooming, abuse, trafficking and modern slavery. I hope that by telling my story it will raise awareness and I can prevent another child from going through what I have.

I decided to cut contact with most of my old friends, although I did see Andrea a year ago. I tried to bury the hatchet, but then I realised that nothing had changed between us and she'd never really been my friend. However, I have stayed in touch with Cola, although she's not in a good place at the moment.

That's why I've written this book. Abuse like this doesn't stop when you reach adulthood. You carry it inside and every day it screams right back at you. It steals your sleep, your confidence and your trust in others. The lasting effects of it stay with you for life, but I want to try to challenge and change this. It is only by talking about CSE, human trafficking and county lines that we can ever hope to erase it. 'County lines' is a term used to describe the transportation of drugs from one area to another by gangs who often use children. The very nature of grooming and CSE and child criminal exploitation (CCE) is to keep secrets. We keep these secrets buried so that we don't talk about them because they are complex and hard to discuss. However, keeping things buried achieves nothing other than to allow criminal behaviour to thrive. We need to start talking to our children. Awareness and education are paramount if we hope to stop exploitation and abuse of the most vulnerable members of our society.

At the time of writing, I'm now in my early thirties. The men and women who abused me all those years ago have left their mark, but they haven't broken my spirit. If anything, going through what I have has only served to make me stronger, more resilient and more determined to stop CSE and CCE. I know people will judge me over the decisions I made in the past, but I was only a child. To be honest, I don't care what people think, but I do care passionately about helping others who have been through what I have.

We need to address the matter of modern slavery. When people think of modern slavery victims they automatically think of immigrants or non-English-speaking people. But I was a victim, and I was born and bred in Wales. I lived in a beautiful area; each year it is packed out with tourists, unaware of what goes on there and in so many other places. I now live happily in a busy city in the south of England. I left Wales because it held far too many bad memories. No one wants to believe horrific things such as CSE and CCE happen to children in the countryside, but they do and they're still happening now. We must help protect all victims, but the system shouldn't be so politically correct and blinkered that it fails to recognise its very own modern slavery victims – we matter too. CSE, CCE and human trafficking are vicious cycles and they need to be broken. Only by recognising that we have a real problem can we ever hope to try and eradicate it.

At some point, when she's much older, I will hand this book to Lily. It is my legacy to her. I have cried countless tears and regretted all the things I've missed out on during my life. All those years were stolen from me and I don't want another child to find themselves in my position. Now is the time to act. If we all pull together then we can break the cycle, eliminate these evil practices and prosecute those responsible. It won't happen overnight, but I refuse to stop until all our children are safe and able to enjoy what they should be entitled to – a normal and happy, carefree childhood.

ADVICE AND INFORMATION

I would like to thank the following organisations which have provided me with advice and invaluable help. Here is a brief description of what they do and how to contact them:

SPACE (Stop & Prevent Adolescent Criminal Exploitation) is an unfunded organisation, influencing national change through partnerships with key players in the CCE (Child Criminal Exploitation) response and providing an unparalleled, free, national service to affected families. Having unprecedented access to the underworld of county lines and CCE, and being intricately well-acquainted with its impact as well as every professional intervention currently available, what is sadly continuingly evident is the general statutory response is ill-equipped and damaging to victims at best, and life-threatening at worst.

Our mission is to improve the current devastating landscape for victims and families by safeguarding, not criminalising, growing numbers of rewired, exploited, groomed, entrenched and entrapped young people; position affected families to navigate the statutory maze with guidance and advocacy whilst being signposted to the potential landmines in their journey; campaign for necessary change in policy and within the Modern Slavery response which currently highlights a disparity impacting UK victims; and prevention and training to equip professionals, parents, and the wider community encountering CCE through a unique combination of professional and personal insight.

You can contact SPACE (www.bespaceaware.co.uk) on:
email@bespaceaware.co.uk
Twitter: @bespaceaware

The Human Trafficking Foundation (HTF) aims to equip parliamentarians, councils and other statutory bodies with issues from the sector and provide tools on how to better respond. For example: The HTF created Trafficking Survivor Care Standards for those charities who support survivors directly; it also created a set of protocols for councils and social workers on how to better identify and support survivors (both are available on the HFT website). The HFT tries to be inclusive – gathering information from those working at a grassroots level and on the frontline – about the changing face of human trafficking and its effects. It supports cross-sector anti-slavery work through an Advisory Forum, the regional National Network Coordinators' Forum, the London Working Group, and the

London Modern Slavery Leads Group, as well as promoting wider public awareness of human trafficking.

For more information, visit the HFT website:
www.humantraffickingfoundation.org
or contact:
info@humantraffickingfoundation.org
Tel 020 3773 2040

Latest NRM statistics released by the Home Office for quarter one: 1 January 2020–31 March 2020.

In this quarter alone, 2,871 potential victims of modern slavery were referred to the NRM – a slight decrease on the previous quarter (believed to be influenced by the effects of restrictions due to the COVID-19 pandemic), but a 33% increase compared to the same quarter in 2019.

Of the 2,871 potential victims:

61% claimed to have been exploited in the UK alone.

Just over half (52%) said they had been exploited as adults, and 43% said they had been exploited as children.

A higher proportion of child potential victims, 833 (67%), claimed they were exploited in the UK only, compared to 851 (57%) of adults.

For child potential victims, criminal exploitation was most common (44%) – with 94% of the perpetrators being male. For those exploited as children, criminal exploitation has been partially driven by an increase in the identification of county lines cases.

Victims from the UK, Albania and Vietnam were the three most common nationalities referred to the NRM.

The majority (92%) were referred to police forces in England for investigation, 4% to Police Scotland, 3% to Welsh police forces and 1% to the Police Service of Northern Ireland.

The term 'modern slavery' includes any form of human trafficking, slavery, servitude or forced labour, as set out in the Modern Slavery Act 2015. Potential victims of modern slavery in the UK are referred to the NRM. Adults (18 years and above) must consent to being referred to the NRM, but children (under 18) do not need consent. NRM referrals can be made by individuals exploited as children who are now adults.

Adults who are given a positive 'reasonable grounds' decision have access to support, including accommodation, subsistence, legal aid and counselling, until a 'conclusive grounds' decision on their case is made. Meanwhile, children are supported by local authorities. Adults with a positive 'conclusive grounds' decision are entitled to at least forty-five days of support to enable them to move on from NRM support. Those with a negative decision receive nine days of support.

All information and figures taken from the Home Office National Referral Mechanism statistics bulletin, dated 2 April 2020.

ACKNOWLEDGEMENTS

There are so many people that I'd like to thank that it's difficult to know where to begin, so I'll start with the most important person – my daughter 'Lily'. You not only saved my life but gave me a reason to carry on when I'd had enough. I am blessed to have such a wonderful daughter. You make me proud every day.

To my lawyer, Silvia Nicolaou Garcia at Simpson Millar – the best human rights lawyer! Thank you, Silvia, for helping me fight to get justice.

Special thanks to my ghostwriter Veronica Clark for penning this book, and for giving me a 'voice' and platform to tell my story. Also, thanks to my literary agents Eve White and Ludo Cinelli for their representation and wise counsel. My special gratitude to Kelly Ellis at HarperCollins Publishers for believing in my story and allowing me to tell it.

Finally, I'd like to give hope to every girl and boy out there who has been exploited, trafficked or abused. Keep fighting, but don't keep silent. I am by your side every step of the way.

MOVING
Memoirs

Stories of hope, courage and
the power of love . . .

Sign up to the Moving Memoirs email and you'll
be the first to hear about new books, discounts,
and get sneak previews from your
favourite authors!

Sign up at

www.moving-memoirs.com